Simran Shah

# Preparation Guide: Redesigned SAT 2016

## *Blue Essay*

Version 1.0

Printed in the United States of America
International Standard Book Number:
978-0-9906704-2-1


Published by Reetiforp, LLC Publishing, a division of Reetiforp, LLC Reetiforp


Publishing books are available at special quantity discounts to
use for sales promotions, employee premiums, or educational purposes.
Please email our Marketing Department to order or for more information at
workbooks@c2educate.com. Please report any errors or corrections
to corrections@c2educate.com.

# Letter to Students and Parents

## To Students and Parents

C2 Education's Redesigned SAT workbooks focus on curriculum that will help students build key foundation skills and learn problem-solving methods to tackle the new SAT to be released in 2016. We strongly recommend that students use these workbooks aligned with instructions and guidance from our tutors at a C2 Education center.

This book contains a number of exercises designed to guide the student through a careful, progressive process that will build layers of understanding and present problems with an increasing degree of difficulty. Each colored (belt) level will confront a variety of topics within the realms of Writing, Essay, Reading, and Math; some topics may re-appear in other workbooks of different difficulties while some topics may only appear once. The ultimate goal of C2 Education's workbooks is to cover the academic content in a comprehensive manner with sufficient practice sets and homework review.

Students will obtain the greatest benefit and improvement from these workbooks by following the workbooks from Lesson 1 to the end. Each lesson will contain the following:

- A diagnostic assessment designed to help our C2 tutors gauge the student's understanding prior to the lesson
- Instructional text and information focused on methodology and problem-solving thought processes
- Practice problems about the concepts presented and any connecting concepts from other lessons
- Test-like practice problems geared to emulate the real exam
- Homework problems to review academic information covered in class and the workbook

We wish you the best of luck in your academic endeavors and we hope that our workbooks will provide you with strong improvements, facilitated understanding, and expanded problem-solving skills. Thank you for being a part of the C2 family; we hope that you enjoy your time learning with us!

- C2 Education's Curriculum Team

# SAT Blue Essay
# Table of Contents

## LESSON eB1 – EVALUATING AN ESSAY

This section will teach you about how the SAT essay is evaluated. Read the lesson and pay close attention to the grading standards for the SAT essay. We'll evaluate several sample essays so that you can get a good idea of what makes a successful (or unsuccessful) SAT essay. At the end, you'll write your first practice essay.

### TOPIC OVERVIEW: THE SAT ESSAY

On the SAT, the essay section is optional. Despite this, it is strongly advised that all students take the SAT essay portion. For a long time, the ACT offered an optional essay, but a lot of colleges – especially top colleges – still required students to provide an essay score. And when it's time to apply to college, it's better to have the essay score and not need it than to need the essay score and not have it.

The SAT essay section is 50 minutes long. The test provides a passage that is between 650 and 750 words long and asks us to evaluate the ways in which the author creates strong, persuasive arguments in the passage.

The essay does **NOT** ask us whether we agree or disagree with the arguments in the passage. Instead, we are asked to analyze the persuasive elements in the passage. This assignment is similar to those seen in many English classes, in which students are asked to analyze an author's use of language, literary elements, or some other facet of writing.

### WHAT DO THE ESSAY PROMPTS LOOK LIKE?

The essay prompt will be the same for every single SAT. Each prompt will look like this:

As you read the passage below, consider how [the author] uses

- evidence, such as facts or examples, to support claims.
- reasoning to develop ideas and to connect claims and evidence.
- stylistic or persuasive elements, such as word choice or appeals to emotion, to add power to the ideas expressed.

*Passage will appear here.*

Write an essay in which you explain how [the author] builds an argument to persuade his or her audience that [author's claim]. In your essay, analyze how [the author] uses one or more of the features listed above (or features of your own choice) to strengthen the logic and persuasiveness of his or her argument. Be sure that your analysis focuses on the most relevant aspects of the passage.

Your essay should not explain whether you agree with [the author's] claims, but rather explain how the author builds an argument to persuade his or her audience.

This is good news because it means that we already know that no matter what the passage is, we will be evaluating an author's use of persuasive techniques to build strong arguments. Many of the lessons in this book will discuss those persuasive techniques.

### WHAT DO ESSAY SCORERS LOOK FOR?

Essay scorers not only evaluate how we write, but also whether the passage was thoroughly understood and how strong the analysis of the author's arguments is. Key grading areas include:

- **Reading Comprehension:**
  - Was the passage fully understood?
  - Does the essay go beyond what the passage explicitly says in order to draw reasonable inferences from the passage?
  - Does the essay demonstrate understanding of the more complex and nuanced ideas in the passage?
- **Focus and Organization:**
  - Does the essay have one clearly stated central claim?
  - Does the essay as a whole focus on that claim?
  - Does the essay flow logically and smoothly from one idea to the next?
- **Analysis and Use of Evidence:**
  - Does the essay analyze the passage in depth or is the analysis superficial?
  - Is evidence from the passage included to support claims made in the essay, and is that evidence used properly and integrated smoothly into the essay?
- **Written Expression:**
  - Is the style formal and informative?
  - Is the use of language precise, high level, and appropriate?
- **Conventions:**
  - Does the essay contain grammar and spelling errors?
  - Do those errors interfere with the reader's understanding of the essay?

One of the best ways to learn how to write a great SAT essay is to look at examples. Today, we'll look at four sample essays written in response to the prompt on the following page. For each essay, use the lines provided to make comments, corrections, and notes. While you read each essay, keep the grading areas in mind because you're going to score each essay afterwards.

**Directions:** Read the essay prompt below. While you read the passage, use the lines provided to make notes about the author's use of evidence, reasoning, and other persuasive elements to build his arguments.

As you read the passage below, consider how Dana Gioia uses

- evidence, such as facts or examples, to support claims.
- reasoning to develop ideas and to connect claims and evidence.
- stylistic or persuasive elements, such as word choice or appeals to emotion, to add power to the ideas expressed.

**Adapted from "Why Literature Matters" by Dana Gioia**
*The New York Times*, **April 10, 2005**

[A] strange thing has happened in the American arts during the past quarter century. While income rose to unforeseen levels, college attendance ballooned, and access to information increased enormously, the interest young Americans showed in the arts – and especially literature – actually diminished.

According to the 2002 Survey of Public Participation in the Arts, a population study designed and commissioned by the National Endowment for the Arts (and executed by the US Bureau of the Census), arts participation by Americans has declined for eight of the nine major forms that are measured…. The declines have been most severe among younger adults (ages 18-24). The most worrisome finding in the 2002 study, however, is the declining percentage of Americans, especially young adults, reading literature.

That individuals at a time of crucial intellectual and emotional development bypass the joys and challenges of literature is a troubling trend. If it were true that they substituted histories, biographies, or political works for literature, one might not worry. But book reading of any kind is falling as well.

That such a longstanding and fundamental cultural activity should slip so swiftly, especially among young adults, signifies deep transformations in contemporary life. To call attention to the trend, the Arts Endowment issued the reading portion of the Survey as a separate report, "Reading at Risk: A Survey of Literary Reading in America."

The decline in reading has consequences that go beyond literature. The significance of reading has become a persistent theme in the business world. The February issue of *Wired* magazine, for example, sketches a new set of mental skills and habits proper to the 21st century, aptitudes decidedly literary in character: not "linear, logical, analytical talents," author Daniel Pink states, but "the ability to create artistic and emotional beauty, to detect patterns and opportunities, to craft a satisfying narrative." When asked what kind of talents they like to see in management positions,

business leaders consistently set imagination, creativity, and higher-order thinking at the top.

Ironically, the value of reading and the intellectual faculties that it inculcates appear most clearly as active and engaged literacy declines. There is now a growing awareness of the consequences of nonreading to the workplace. In 2001 the National Association of Manufacturers polled its members on skill deficiencies among employees. Among hourly workers, poor reading skills ranked second, and 38 percent of employers complained that local schools inadequately taught reading comprehension.

The decline of reading is also taking its toll in the civic sphere…. A 2003 study of 15- to 26-year-olds' civic knowledge by the National Conference of State Legislatures concluded, "Young people do not understand the ideals of citizenship…and their appreciation and support of American democracy is limited."

It is probably no surprise that declining rates of literary reading coincide with declining levels of historical and political awareness among young people. One of the surprising findings of "Reading at Risk" was that literary readers are markedly more civically engaged than nonreaders, scoring two to four times more likely to perform charity work, visit a museum, or attend a sporting event. One reason for their higher social and cultural interactions may lie in the kind of civic and historical knowledge that comes with literary reading….

The evidence of literature's importance to civic, personal, and economic health is too strong to ignore. The decline of literary reading foreshadows serious long-term social and economic problems, and it is time to bring literature and the other arts into discussions of public policy. Libraries, schools, and public agencies do noble work, but addressing the reading issue will require the leadership of politicians and the business community as well….

Reading is not a timeless, universal capability. Advanced literacy is a specific intellectual skill and social habit that depends on a great many educational, cultural, and economic factors. As more Americans lose this capability, our nation becomes less informed, active, and independent-minded. These are not the qualities that a free, innovative, or productive society can afford to lose.

Write an essay in which you explain how Dana Gioia builds an argument to persuade his audience that the decline of reading in America will have a negative effect on society. In your essay, analyze how Gioia uses one or more of the features listed above (or features of your own choice) to strengthen the logic and persuasiveness of his argument. Be sure that your analysis focuses on the most relevant features of the passage.

Your essay should not explain whether you agree with Gioia's claims, but rather explain how Gioia builds an argument to persuade his audience.

**Directions:** Carefully read each essay. While you read, pretend that you are looking over a friend's essay. Use the lines provided to make comments, suggestions, critiques, and other notes. Pay particular attention to the key grading areas: Reading comprehension, focus and organization, analysis and evidence, written expression, and conventions.

**SAMPLE ESSAY A**

Dana Gioia, author of "Why Literature Matters," is a very persuasive writer. In this articl, he uses powerful word choices to appeal to emotions, as well as using several pieces of evidence to support his various arguments. As a result, "Why Literature Matters" is a very persuasive article that argues that we must do something to encourage young people to read more for the good of the country.

Citing "Reading at Risk," a study by the National Endowment for the Arts, Gioia points out that Americans in general are reading less, especially young Americans. Though this isn't really an argument more just a statement of a fact, Gioia has to establish the decline in reading for his future arguments to make any sense. Gioia uses powerful persuasive language to create a sense of urgency around the decline in reading. By saying that reading is a "fundamental cultural activity", he makes reading seem very important to the nation as a whole. By suggesting that it may well slip away, he creates a sense of urgency that suggests that we must act before reading is gone entirely.

Gioia's main arguements involve the possible widespread impacts of a decline in reading, especially economic and civic impacts. In explaining the economic impacts, Gioia relies on several sources of evidence. First, he uses an article from *Wired* magazine that says the skills needed in 21st century jobs are skills that can be gained from reading. He supports this with a survey of business leaders who claims that they look for imagination and creativity in managers. So, according to Gioia's evidence, people must read in order to succeed in business.

Gioia takes his argument past the business world by pointing out a poll of members of the National Association of Manufacturers. In the poll, members said that their employee's lack of reading skills was a big problem and blamed the schools for not teaching reading comprehension. This piece of evidence is important because it suggests that even hourly factory workers need to be able to read to do well at their jobs. So not reading is

bad for people in almost any job.

Next, Gioia argues that a decline in reading also has civic impacts. He cites a study that shows that young people don't know what it means to be a good citizen. But this does not have any real link to reading. To link this to reading, Gioia refers to "Reading at Risk," which found that people who read are more likely to volunteer and be involved in their communities. Gioia uses this evidence to suggest that reading is important for people to be civic minded because reading teaches them about important parts of citizenship like history.

Finally, Gioia closes with an appeal to his audience's emotions. He says that a nation that's supposed to be free and innovative can't do that without having a well read population, which appeals to people's sense of pride and patriotism. Because of this wording Gioia closes his article on a very strong note and helps to make his other arguments stronger.

## SAMPLE ESSAY B

Authors often use a variety of elements to create strong arguements, and several of these persuasive elements can be seen in "Why Literature Matters" by Dana Gioia. Gioia creates his arguments by using a wide variety of evidence and persuasive language to appeal to his readers and create a sense of urgency.

Gioia begins by explaining that Americans do not read as much as they used to. Rather than expecting his readers to take his word for it, Gioia points to a study by the National Endowment for the Arts called "Reading at Risk: A Survey of Literary Reading in America," which found that fewer Americans read now than in the past, a trend that is especially noticeable among young Americans. By citing a survey conducting by such a reputable source, Gioia is able to easily establish the current problem.

The fact that fewer Americans read now than in the past is not necessarily alarming. Gioia attempts to create a sense of urgency regarding the situation by using emotional language. He calls reading a "longstanding and fundamental cultural activity," which establishes reading as a basic part of our culture. By claiming that it is "slip[ping] so swiftly," he creates a sense of urgency in suggesting that if we don't act, reading may not be around for much longer.

To convince his audience that a decline in reading is a very big problem, Gioia argues that a lack of reading could have economic and civic consequences. In explaining the potential economic consequences, Gioia relies on evidence from multiple sources. He quotes from an article in *Wired* magazine in order to explain that jobs in the future will require skills that can only be gained by reading. This piece of evidence could have been stronger if Gioia had given his audience some information about *Wired* and why it is a good source but Gioia backs his claims up with further evidence. He cites a survey of business leaders that found that these leaders look for imagination and creativity – which can be gained from reading – in managers. He also cites a poll by the National Association of Manufacturers that found that most members blame schools for not teaching reading

comprehension to their employees. Because he provides this more number-based evidence this is one of Gioia's strongest arguments. After all, numbers don't lie.

In addition to economic problems, a lack of reading could cause civic problems, according to Gioia. This is Gioia's weakest argument because he doesn't really provide a lot of evidence to back up his claim. He does note a study that found that young people don't understand what it means to be a good citizen, but that has nothing to do with reading. The only way he links civic engagement and reading is by saying that "Reading at Risk" found that people who read more are also more likely to go to museums or volunteer. But this does not really prove that reading makes people better citizens.

Despite this somewhat weak argument, Gioia ends the article on a strong note. In the last two sentences of the article, he appeals to his audiences patriotism and pride while also creating a sense of fear and urgency: "As more Americans lose this capability, our nation becomes less informed, active, and independent-minded. These are not the qualities that a free, innovative, or productive society can afford to lose." Though he provides no evidence, these two sentences use such strong language that they help to make all of Gioia's other arguments stronger.

## SAMPLE ESSAY C

In "Why Literature Matters," author Dana Gioia argues that declining interest in reading, particularly among young Americans, could have far-reaching consequences that extend far beyond the arts. Gioia's arguments rest on a variety of evidence drawn from reputable sources and are further developed by Gioia's skillful use of language to evoke an emotional response from readers.

In order to argue that a lack of reading may cause widespread problems in the future, Gioia must first establish that there is actually a decline in reading among Americans. He does this by relying on a study by the National Endowment for the Arts, "Reading at Risk: A Survey of Literary Reading in America." Had Gioia simply stated that Americans read less today than they did in the past, he would have left room for readers to doubt the severity of the problem, which would make the rest of Gioia's arguments less powerful.

To underscore the urgency of the problem, Gioia employs powerful language. In calling reading a "longstanding and fundamental cultural activity," Gioia encourages his audience to share his dismay over reading's lack of popularity. In saying that reading has "slip[ped] so swiftly," Gioia creates a greater sense of urgency, suggesting that literature may well disappear if we do not act. This language, in combination with the data provided from "Reading at Risk", helps to make the reader feel more strongly about Gioia's arguments.

After establishing that the decline in reading is indeed a problem, Gioia focuses on exploring the extent of the problem.

He begins by discussing the potential economic problems caused by a lack of reading. Gioia quotes from a *Wired* magazine article that argued that the skills necessary for success in the 21st century workplace require literary talents such as creativity. This is Gioia's weakest piece of evidence because it relies on the reader's familiarity with *Wired* magazine. If the reader does not know whether *Wired* is a reputable source, the quotes from the article carry little weight. The argument is made stronger by Gioia's use of additional evidence, including a survey of business leaders who claim to value imagination and a poll of

members of the National Association of Manufacturers who cite poor reading skills as a primary problem in the workplace. These more quantifiable sources help to make Gioia's argument far stronger than if it relied solely on the article from *Wired*.

In addition to the economic impacts of a decline in reading, Gioia discusses the civic impacts, arguing that a decline in reading results in a decline in civic engagement. This is Gioia's weakest argument in that it relies on a single piece of evidence that draws a correlation rather than a cause and effect relationship. Gioia cites "Reading at Risk", which found that those who read are more likely to volunteer, visit museums, or attend sporting events. Although Gioia suggests a reason for this relationship between reading and civic engagement – that reading provides civic and historical knowledge – this does not truly establish that reading definitely creates more involved citizens.

Finally, Gioia ties his arguments together to assert that the potential impacts of a decline in literacy are far too great to ignore. Here, he relies almost exclusively on the power of words, closing his article by appealing to the reader's patriotism: "These are not the qualities that a free, innovative, or productive society can afford to lose."

## SAMPLE ESSAY D

The Greek philosopher Aristotle divided the means of persuasion into three categories: Ethos, pathos, and logos. Any persuasive writer must incorporate these tools into his arsenal, as Dana Gioia has clearly done in "Why Literature Matters". Using the concepts of ethos (ethical appeals), pathos (emotional appeals), and logos (logical appeals), Gioia constructs three interrelated arguments to conclude that the declining importance of literature in American society may well undermine the very fabric of our country.

Gioia begins by arguing that declining literacy is most severe among young Americans, relying almost exclusively on logical, evidence-based appeals that rest on the findings of "Reading at Risk: A Survey of Literary Reading in America". However, in establishing the significance of this trend, Gioia branches beyond logos to make a more emotional appeal. By defining reading as a "longstanding and fundamental cultural activity," Gioia seeks an emotional response from readers who, given that they are readers, will likely share Gioia's dismay over the decline of literature.

Having established that declining literacy among young Americans is indeed a problem, Gioia begins to argue the breadth and significance of the problem. According to Gioia, declines in reading may have economic and civic impacts that could undermine the very principles on which our nation was founded.

In explaining the potential economic impacts of a widespread decline in reading, Gioia utilizes both logical and ethical appeals. He begins by referencing an article in *Wired* magazine, a publication known for its attention to trends in the world of technology. Though Gioia does not cite specific data from the article, he quotes the article's author, Daniel Pink, extensively. As readers, we are expected to give Pink's words greater weight than Gioia's because Pink specializes in writing about business and technology. Thus the evidence Gioia uses here rests primarily on the reader's opinion of Pink as a credible source of information, placing this argument into the category of ethos. In case Pink's testimony is insufficient, Gioia again relies on data driven evidence, citing a poll in which members of the National

Association of Manufacturers reported that their employees lacked fundamental reading comprehension skills.

To establish the potential civic impacts of declines in reading, Gioia relies primarily on logical appeals, citing evidence from two studies, including "Reading at Risk." The first study, by the National Conference of State Legislatures, concluded that today's youth lack understanding and appreciation for the ideals of citizenship. The findings from "Reading at Risk" establish that those who read are more likely to be civically engaged. The two studies taken together suggest that civic engagement stems, at least in part, from reading, thus establishing that the decline in reading may be to blame for the decline in civic engagement.

Gioia concludes his article by connecting these three arguments together. That reading declines are most prevalent among young Americans suggests that this trend is likely to continue into the future, as these youth grow into the adults who drive the nation. That reading declines have both economic and civic impacts suggests that a continued decline in reading could have far-reaching impacts, resulting in a nation that "becomes less informed, active, and independent-minded."

By utilizing all three forms of persuasive reasoning and relying on a wide variety of data-driven evidence, Gioia creates a strong argument in favor of acting to halt and reverse the decline of reading in the U.S.

## HOMEWORK

**Directions:** On this page and the next page, you'll see a rubric for grading SAT essays. This rubric is based on the grading standards for scoring SAT essays. You're going to put yourself in the shoes of an essay grader and give scores for each of the sample essays you read in class. For each essay, you'll give a score for Reading Comprehension, Focus and Organization, Analysis and Use of Evidence, Written Expression, and Conventions. Then you'll give the essay an overall score and write comments to explain your score.

|  | 4 | 3 | 2 | 1 | 0 |
|---|---|---|---|---|---|
| **Reading Comprehension** | • Accurate analysis of what the text says explicitly and inferentially<br>• Full comprehension of complex ideas in the source text | • Mostly accurate analysis of what the text says explicitly and inferentially<br>• Extensive comprehension of the ideas expressed in the text | • Generally accurate analysis of what the text says explicitly, though inferences may be somewhat inaccurate<br>• Basic comprehension of the ideas in the text | • Minimally accurate analysis of what the text says explicitly<br>• Minimal comprehension of the ideas expressed in the text | • Provides an inaccurate analysis or no analysis of the text<br>• Shows little to no comprehension of the ideas expressed in the text |
| **Focus and Organization** | • Central claim is clearly stated, focused, and strongly maintained<br>• Consistent use of a variety of transitional strategies<br>• Logical progression of ideas from beginning to end<br>• Includes a strong introduction and conclusion | • Central claim is clear and mostly maintained, though some loosely related material may be present<br>• Adequate use of transitional strategies with some variety<br>• Adequate progression of ideas from beginning to end<br>• Incudes an adequate introduction and conclusion | • Central claim may be somewhat unclear or unfocused<br>• Central claim may be clear, but is insufficiently maintained<br>• Inconsistent use of transitional strategies and/or little variety<br>• Uneven progression of ideas from beginning to end<br>• Weak introduction and conclusion, if any | • Central claim may be confusing or ambiguous<br>• Central claim may be somewhat clear, but poorly maintained<br>• Few or no transitional strategies<br>• Frequent extraneous ideas may intrude<br>• Unclear progression of ideas<br>• May be lacking introduction or conclusion | • May be inappropriate to task, purpose, and/or audience<br>• Lack of any coherence, clarity, or cohesion<br>• May be off-topic or illegible |
| **Analysis and Use of Evidence** | • Response analyzes source text in substantial depth and specificity<br>• Use of evidence is integrated, comprehensive, relevant, and concrete | • Response analyzes source text in some depth and specificity but is predominantly general<br>• Adequate evidence is included in the response, but citations may be imprecise and evidence may not be well integrated | • Response provides uneven, cursory analysis that achieves little depth<br>• Some evidence is included, but it is not properly cited or integrated into the response | • Response provides minimal analysis of the source text<br>• Use of evidence is minimal, absent, incorrect, or irrelevant | • Analysis is wholly inaccurate or incomplete<br>• No evidence is provided |

| | | | | | |
|---|---|---|---|---|---|
| **Written Expression** | • Establishes and maintains a formal and informative style<br>• Uses precise language consistently, including descriptive words and phrases, linking and transitional words, and words to indicate tone | • Establishes and maintains an effective style<br>• Uses mostly precise language, including descriptive words and phrases, linking and transitional words, and words to indicate tone | • Establishes and mostly maintains an appropriate style<br>• Uses some precise language, though language use may be inconsistent | • Fails to maintain an appropriate style or establishes a style that has limited effectiveness<br>• Includes limited descriptions, details, linking or transitional words, or words to indicate tone | • Inappropriate style<br>• No precise language |
| **Conventions** | • Few, if any, errors in grammar and usage<br>• No errors that interfere with meaning<br>• No systematic pattern of errors | • Some errors in grammar and usage<br>• Some errors may be distracting, but meaning remains clear | • Several errors in grammar and usage<br>• Some errors may impede understanding<br>• Patterns of errors are evident | • Multiple errors in grammar and usage<br>• Multiple distracting errors that may impede understanding<br>• Patterns of errors are evident | • Essay demonstrates little to no command of the conventions of Standard English |

**Sample Essay A**

| | |
|---|---|
| Reading Comprehension: | _____ / 4 |
| Focus and Organization: | _____ / 4 |
| Analysis and Use of Evidence: | _____ / 4 |
| Written Expression: | _____ / 4 |
| Conventions: | _____ / 4 |

*Overall Score:*     _____ / 4

Explain your scores using complete sentences:

_____

_____

_____

_____

_____

_____

_____

_____

**Sample Essay B**

Reading Comprehension:                _____ / 4

Focus and Organization:                _____ / 4

Analysis and Use of Evidence:        _____ / 4

Written Expression:                        _____ / 4

Conventions:                                  _____ / 4

*Overall Score:*                              _____ */ 4*

Explain your scores using complete sentences:

_____

_____

_____

_____

_____

_____

_____

_____

Unauthorized copying or reuse of any part of this page is illegal.

**Sample Essay C**

Reading Comprehension: _____ / 4

Focus and Organization: _____ / 4

Analysis and Use of Evidence: _____ / 4

Written Expression: _____ / 4

Conventions: _____ / 4

*Overall Score:* _____ / 4

Explain your scores using complete sentences:

_____

_____

_____

_____

_____

_____

_____

_____

**Sample Essay D**

Reading Comprehension:          _____ / 4

Focus and Organization:          _____ / 4

Analysis and Use of Evidence:    _____ / 4

Written Expression:              _____ / 4

Conventions:                     _____ / 4


*Overall Score:*                 _____ / 4


Explain your scores using complete sentences:

_____

_____

_____

_____

_____

_____

_____

_____

## LESSON eB2 – EVALUATING ARGUMENTS

In this section, we will work on identifying and evaluating an author's arguments and the support the author provides for those arguments. This is a key skill for success on the SAT essay.

### TOPIC OVERVIEW: EVALUATING ARGUMENTS

The SAT essay asks us to explain how an author builds arguments in a given passage. To do this, we will need to be able to identify and evaluate arguments and the ways in which the author supports his or her claims.

The SAT essay prompt will tell us to consider how the author uses evidence, reasoning, and stylistic or persuasive elements. In this lesson, we will focus primarily on **reasoning** and **evidence**, as these are the two primary ways in which authors support their arguments.

### IDENTIFYING ARGUMENTS

In the last lesson, we looked at the way the essay prompt is structured. After the passage, the essay prompt will tell us the author's primary argument.

*Tip: Read the part of the prompt that follows the passage BEFORE you read the passage itself.*

If we already know the author's primary claim, it's much easier to identify supporting arguments. Let's consider the sample prompt from the previous lesson. The prompt told us that the author was claiming that the decline in reading would have a negative effect on society. Knowing that, we can examine the passage for arguments that explain what the negative effects might be – in this case, the negative effects would be a workforce that is ill-prepared for the demands of the modern workplace and a population that is not civically engaged.

*Tip: While reading the passage, underline sentences that might provide supporting arguments for the author's main claim.*

### IDENTIFYING SUPPORT

Once we've identified an author's arguments, we need to look at how the author supports those arguments. Authors will usually support arguments by providing some form of evidence for the argument and by using logical reasoning to link the evidence to the argument itself. Let's look at an example:

> It is probably no surprise that declining rates of literary reading coincide with declining levels of historical and political awareness among young people. One of the surprising findings of "Reading at Risk" was that literary readers are markedly more civically engaged than nonreaders, scoring two to four times more likely to perform charity work, visit a museum, or attend a sporting event. One reason for their higher social and cultural interactions may lie in the kind of civic and historical knowledge that comes with literary reading.

This paragraph is just three sentences long, yet it contains an argument, evidence, and logical reasoning linking that evidence to the argument. The first sentence ("It is…young people") provides the argument. The second sentence ("One of…sporting event") provides evidence. The third sentence ("One reason…reading") provides logical reasoning to link the evidence with the argument.

Evidence will typically have a source affiliated with it. This might be an authoritative group or publication; the name of a study, survey, or poll; or the name of a group that conducted a study, survey, or poll.

*Tip: To identify evidence, look for a clearly identified source. Key phrases like "according to," "findings of," or "found" can help pinpoint specific pieces of evidence.*

## PRACTICE WITH ARGUMENTS

**Directions:** Each of the following paragraphs contains an argument that includes evidence and logical reasoning. As with the example on the previous page, identify the main argument, the evidence, and the logical reasoning.

1.  Though generally intended to curb violent crime rates, strict gun control laws are actually harmful to the citizenry. During the years in which the Washington, D.C. handgun ban, one of the most stringent gun control policies in the nation, was in effect, the D.C. murder rate averaged 73% higher than it had been at the time the law was passed. Similar trends have been seen in cities such as Chicago, which also banned handguns, suggesting that strictly limiting gun ownership rights takes guns away from those who would use them for defense, leaving illegal weapons in the hands of those who use them to commit violence.

    Summarize the argument:

    _____
    _____

    Summarize the evidence:

    _____
    _____

    Summarize the reasoning:

    _____
    _____

2.  Though many pet owners may disagree, it is in the public's best interest to pass and enforce laws that require that pets be spayed or neutered. Many communities suffer from severe pet over-population, resulting in declining home values, increased traffic accidents, and higher rates of dog-bite incidents, all of which cost insurance companies – and, by extension, those they insure – millions of dollars per year. Pet over-population is best addressed by enforcing spay/neuter laws that prevent unwanted litters from being born.

    Summarize the argument:

    _____
    _____

    Summarize the evidence:

    _____
    _____

    Summarize the reasoning:

    _____
    _____

## EVALUATING EVIDENCE

If we are going to explain how an author built an argument, it's a good idea to focus on the author's strongest pieces of evidence. To do that, we need to be able to distinguish strong evidence from weaker evidence. Let's begin by looking at some types of evidence you might find in SAT essay passages:

- **Authorities**: This kind of evidence usually involves quoting or referencing an expert. To identify this kind of support, look for phrases like "according to __source__." The strength of the evidence depends on how credible the authority is. For instance, in supporting an argument about the value of early childhood education, a quote from a developmental psychologist would carry more weight than a quote from a parent. The parent's knowledge would come solely from his or her specific parenting experiences, while the psychologist's knowledge would come from years of research and study.
- **Anecdotal Evidence:** This kind of evidence usually comes from either the author's personal experiences or from the experiences of others. For example, if an author is arguing that support for the homeless is insufficient, he might share the story of a homeless person. This type of evidence tends to rely on emotion over logic. That one person's experience might be heartbreaking, but it also may not be representative of the experiences of all homeless people. While anecdotes can be very persuasive, they are not usually considered as strong as other forms of evidence.
- **Studies or Research:** This evidence is generally considered the strongest kind of evidence. Published research tends to be free of bias, based on a large sample size, and grounded in objective numbers. That said, the value of research rests, at least in part, on the credibility of the researchers. For example, if an author is arguing that green energy will not truly help to prevent climate change, research done by General Electric or Exxon Mobile would be less valuable than research from an independent group. Likewise, facts that are stated without any source given are less powerful than facts that are attributed to a source.

*Tip: While you read the passage, make notes in the margins about the types of evidence you find. This will make it easier to reference the author's use of evidence when you write your essay.*

## EVALUATING EVIDENCE-BASED ARGUMENTS

In later lessons, we will explore arguments that do not rest on evidence, such as emotional appeals, but many of the arguments included in essay passages will rely on evidence that is linked to the argument by logical reasoning. When evaluating evidence-based arguments, we must look at all three parts: the argument itself (the claim), the evidence, and the logic that connects the evidence to the argument. When evaluating arguments, consider:

- *What is the argument or claim?*
- *What is the evidence supporting the claim?*
- *Is the evidence strong? Does it come from a credible source? Is it subjective or objective?*
- *Is there a clear link between the evidence and the argument?*
- *Does the author's logical reasoning make perfect sense, or is the author making assumptions in linking the evidence to the argument?*

## PRACTICE WITH ARGUMENTS

**Directions:** For each paragraph, answer the questions provided. Some of these questions are based on your opinion of the author's argument. You should provide reasons for your opinion, just as you would need to in an SAT essay.

We must resist any effort to allow the government to censor entertainment. Freedom of speech and media are essential to a democratic form of government. As Benjamin Franklin wrote, "Whoever would overthrow the liberty of a nation must begin by subduing the freeness of speech." If we allow the government to limit speech in the form of entertainment, we will take the first step down a path toward authoritarianism.

1. What is the author's primary claim or argument?

   _____

   _____

2. What kind of evidence (authority, anecdote, or study/research) does the author provide?

   _____

3. In your opinion, is this evidence strong? Why or why not?

   _____

   _____

   _____

   _____

4. Describe how the author links the evidence to the argument.

   _____

   _____

   _____

   _____

5. In your opinion, is this a strong argument? Why or why not?

   _____

   _____

   _____

   _____

6. What could the author do to make this argument stronger?

   _____

   _____

   _____

   _____

Lately we have begun to recognize that we are poisoning ourselves with our lawns, which receive more pesticides and herbicides per acre than any crop grown in this country. These chemicals pose risks to both the environment and our health. In fact, the National Coalition for Pesticide Free Lawns reports that 19 of the 30 most commonly used lawn pesticides are linked with cancer. For the good of our world and ourselves, we must explore alternatives to chemically treated lawns.

7.   What is the author's primary claim or argument?

_____

_____

8.   What kind of evidence (authority, anecdote, or study/research) does the author provide?

_____

9.   In your opinion, is this evidence strong? Why or why not?

_____

_____

_____

_____

10.  Describe how the author links the evidence to the argument.

_____

_____

_____

_____

11.  In your opinion, is this a strong argument? Why or why not?

_____

_____

_____

_____

12.  What could the author do to make this argument stronger?

_____

_____

_____

_____

In order to preserve our interactions with nature and with other people, we must make efforts to limit our own digital connectivity. The ubiquity of smart phones has been a boon to many areas of modern life, but it has eroded our ability to appreciate the world and the people around us. For decades, I have walked the same Cape Cod dunes that Thoreau once walked. Once, people walked with their heads up, looking at the water, the sky, the sand, and one another. Now they walk with their heads down, typing.

13. What is the author's primary claim or argument?

_____

_____

14. What kind of evidence (authority, anecdote, or study/research) does the author provide?

_____

15. In your opinion, is this evidence strong? Why or why not?

_____

_____

_____

_____

16. Describe how the author links the evidence to the argument.

_____

_____

_____

_____

17. In your opinion, is this a strong argument? Why or why not?

_____

_____

_____

_____

18. What could the author do to make this argument stronger?

_____

_____

_____

_____

We cannot hope to improve the criminal justice system without addressing minimum sentencing rules, which often require harsh penalties for relatively minor, non-violent crimes. Though many argue that mandatory minimum sentences are necessary in order to control crime, several states, including South Carolina, Ohio, and Rhode Island, have actually seen crime rates remain the same or lower after reducing mandatory minimum sentences. Such changes have far reaching effects on the entire justice system, lowering prison populations, reducing the costs of frequent appeals, and allowing states to focus on rehabilitation over prosecution.

19. What is the author's primary claim or argument?

_____

_____

20. What kind of evidence (authority, anecdote, or study/research) does the author provide?

_____

21. In your opinion, is this evidence strong? Why or why not?

_____

_____

_____

_____

22. Describe how the author links the evidence to the argument.

_____

_____

_____

_____

23. In your opinion, is this a strong argument? Why or why not?

_____

_____

_____

_____

24. What could the author do to make this argument stronger?

_____

_____

_____

_____

**Directions:** Read the essay prompt below. While you read the passage, use the lines provided to make notes about the author's use of evidence, reasoning, and other persuasive elements to build his arguments.

As you read the passage below, consider how Yudhijit Bhattacharjee uses

- evidence, such as facts or examples, to support claims.
- reasoning to develop ideas and to connect claims and evidence.
- stylistic or persuasive elements, such as word choice or appeals to emotion, to add power to the ideas expressed.

**Adapted from "Why Bilinguals Are Smarter" by Yudhijit Bhattacharjee**
*The New York Times*, March 18, 2012

Speaking two languages has clear practical benefits in an increasingly globalized world, but in recent years, scientists have begun to provide that the advantages of bilingualism are even more fundamental than being able to converse with a broader range of people. Their research suggests that being bilingual actually makes a person smarter, raising interesting questions for the future of education in the United States.

This new perspective on bilingualism represents a stark contrast against previous views of bilingualism. Through much of the 20th century, researchers and educators considered a second language to be a cognitive interference that hindered a child's academic and intellectual development. In fact, the only reason that many public schools implemented bilingual education in the 20th century was to help immigrant students transition into English-only classrooms.

It is true that a second language creates interference. Neuroscientists have found that in a bilingual's brain, both language systems are active even when only one language is being used, which can create situations in which one language system obstructs the other. Recent research, however, has found that this interference is more of a blessing than a handicap because is forces the brain to resolve internal conflict, thereby strengthening cognitive ability.

A 2004 study by psychologists Ellen Bialystok and Michelle Martin-Rhee suggests that this heightened ability translates into greater problem solving abilities. In the study, bilingual and monolingual preschoolers were asked to sort blue circles and red squares presented on a computer screen into digital bins marked with a blue square and a red circle. In the first task, the children were asked to sort the shapes by color. Both groups did this with relative ease. Next, the children were asked to sort by shape, which required placing the images in a bin marked with a conflicting color. On this more challenging task, bilinguals were far faster and more accurate.

The collective evidence from a number of similar studies suggests that bilingual abilities improve the brain's executive function, the command system that controls the processes for planning, problem solving, and performing several other mentally demanding tasks. Until recently,

researchers believed that this bilingual advantage came from the brain's ability to suppress one language system. It was thought that this suppression helped to train the brain to ignore distractions. Further studies, however, have shown that bilinguals perform better than monolinguals even at tasks that do not require suppression, suggesting that there is something more at work in the bilingual brain.

The key difference between bilinguals and monolinguals may be more basic: a heightened ability to monitor the environment. "Bilinguals have to switch languages quite often," says Albert Costa, a researcher at the University of Pompeu Fabra in Spain. "This requires keeping track of changes around you in the same way that we monitor our surroundings when driving." In a study comparing German-Italian bilinguals with Italian monolinguals on monitoring tasks, Mr. Costa found that the bilinguals not only performed better, but did so with less activity in parts of the brain involved in monitoring, suggesting that they were more efficient at it.

The bilingual experience also appears to influence the brain from infancy to old age. In a 2009 study led by Agnes Kovacs of the International School for Advanced Studies in Italy, 7-month-old babies exposed to two languages from birth were compared with babies raised with one language. In a series of trials, the bilingual babies were able to learn to anticipate the appearance of a puppet much faster than the monolingual babies. A separate study showed that bilingualism's effect extends into old age. This study, led by neuropsychologist Tamar Gollan of the University of California, San Diego, examined 44 Spanish-English bilinguals and found that individuals who were more proficient in both languages were more resistant than others to the onset of dementia: The higher the person's degree of bilingualism, the later the age of dementia of Alzheimer's onset.

Toward the latter part of the 20th century, many states began to move away from bilingual education, emphasizing English-immersion for immigrant students and limiting opportunities for native English speakers to learn a second language. With this new research in mind, it may be time to reexamine the benefits of bilingual education for all, an initiative that has the potential to improve the cognitive function of entire generations of students. In an increasingly global – and multilingual – world, can we really afford to remain a nation of monolinguals?

Write an essay in which you explain how Yudhijit Bhattacharjee builds an argument to persuade his audience of the benefits of bilingualism and its potential role in education. In your essay, analyze how Bhattacharjee uses one or more of the features listed above (or features of your own choice) to strengthen the logic and persuasiveness of his argument. Be sure that your analysis focuses on the most relevant features of the passage.

Your essay should not explain whether you agree with Bhattacharjee's claims, but rather explain how Bhattacharjee builds an argument to persuade his audience.

**HOMEWORK**

**Directions:** Using the essay prompt you analyzed in class, write a practice SAT essay. Since you are doing this for homework, you will not be timed, but to test your ability to write a good essay under realistic conditions, you should try to limit your writing time to no more than 30 minutes.

_____
_____
_____
_____
_____
_____
_____
_____
_____
_____
_____
_____
_____
_____
_____
_____
_____
_____
_____
_____
_____
_____
_____
_____
_____
_____
_____
_____
_____
_____

## LESSON EB3 – ANNOTATING PASSAGES

In this section, we will learn to annotate a passage for an essay prompt. Using some of your essay time to annotate the passage will help you to write a much stronger SAT essay.

### TOPIC OVERVIEW: ANNOTATING PASSAGES

Annotating is a way of describing the process of making notes and comments on something. We might annotate a textbook, a poem, or – in the case of the SAT essay – a persuasive article.

When annotating a passage, make a lot of notes and comments in the margins. Although notes should be limited to comments that identify and evaluate the author's arguments, use of persuasive elements, and word choices, it is a good idea to include more notes than could possibly be addressed in an essay; this helps to provide ample discussion material, which makes writing the essay a much faster, smoother process.

By annotating the passage, we are forced to actively engage the article, which helps us to pick up on the small details of the author's style and arguments. Annotating also helps us to:

- focus on the task at hand.
- gain greater understanding of the passage.
- plan your essay while reading.
- locate significant quotes to use in your essay.

The *only* way to write a strong SAT essay within the given time limits will be to multitask – annotating kills two birds with one stone by allowing us to simultaneously read the passage and begin planning the essay.

### BEFORE WE BEGIN

> *Tip: Read the part of the prompt that follows the passage BEFORE you read the passage itself.*

Remember that this allows us to identify the author's main argument before reading the passage, which helps us to better identify supporting arguments.

### WHAT TO LOOK FOR

When annotating a passage, remember the phrasing of the prompt. The prompt itself guides us in identify important elements of the passage by telling us that we need to make note of:

- Evidence, such as facts or examples, to support claims.
- Reasoning to develop ideas and to connect claims and evidence.
- Stylistic or persuasive elements, such as word choice or appeals to emotion, to add power to the ideas expressed.

### EVIDENCE

We talked about how to evaluate evidence in our last lesson so let's review. The three kinds of evidence that we discussed in the last lesson were:

- **Authorities:** Quotes or references to experts. Look for phrases like "according to so-and-so." Can be very good evidence, depending on the credibility of the expert.
- **Anecdotes:** Usually reference the experiences of the author or another person. Can be very persuasive, but not usually considered as strong as other evidence because they are subjective and limited in scope.
- **Studies or Research:** Usually considered the most objective kind of evidence. Look for words like "findings" or "reported." Remember to look for the source of the information – some sources can be better than others.

## REASONING

It's not enough for an author to simply state his claim and provide some evidence. The author must also provide logical reasoning that clearly links the evidence to the claim. Let's look at a quick example:

*Censorship cannot be allowed to gain footing in a free and democratic society. For example, in Hitler's Germany, mass book burnings were held to destroy any material contrary to the ideals of the Nazi Party. This helped to suppress resistance against the Nazi government.*

It feels like something is missing here, doesn't it? The author gave us a claim and some evidence, but he didn't clearly explain the link between the two. Although we can probably fill in the blanks ourselves, a reader should never need to make assumptions for an argument to be valid. Look at the example again, this time with logical reasoning added:

*Censorship cannot be allowed to gain footing in a free and democratic society. <u>Censorship can too easily lead to government control over ideas, resulting in a society that values conformity over all else</u>. For example, in Hitler's Germany, mass book burnings were held to destroy any materials contrary to the ideals of the Nazi Party. This helped to suppress resistance against the Nazi government.*

In this example, we only added one sentence, but now the entire argument is much stronger. That one sentence provides the link between the author's evidence and the author's claim.

## STYLISTIC OR PERSUASIVE ELEMENTS

Authors often use specific words, sentence structures, imagery, analogies, metaphors, or tones in order to persuade readers. Sometimes an author's words are chosen to create an emotional response that makes the reader more likely to agree with the author. Other times, the author chooses particular words or sentence structures to add power to his arguments.

In a later lesson, we'll examine this concept in more depth. For today, let's look at a couple of quick examples:

> *__I have a dream__ that my four little children will one day live in a nation where they will not be judged by the color of their skin but by the content of their character. __I have a dream today__. I __have a dream__ that one day, down in Alabama, little black boys and black girls will be able to join hands with little white boys and white girls as sisters and brothers. __I have a dream today__.*

This is excerpted from Martin Luther King, Jr.'s famous "I Have a Dream" speech. His <u>repetition</u> of "I have a dream" makes the speech more memorable, and therefore more persuasive. Authors often use repetition to emphasize key ideas.

> *We have come to dedicate a portion of that field, as a final resting place for __those who here gave their lives that the nation might live__…. The world will little note, __nor long remember what we say here, but it can never forget what they did here.__*

This is an excerpt from The Gettysburg Address. Here we see the use of <u>contrast</u>, in which the author draws a clear contrast in order to help emphasize a point. Lincoln contrasted the men dying and the nation surviving in order to emphasize the significance of the dead soldiers' sacrifices.

> *But even if we pass this [civil rights] bill, the __battle__ will not be over. What happened in Selma is part of a far larger movement which reaches into __every section and State of America__. It is the effort of [African Americans] to secure for themselves the __full blessings of American life__. __Their cause must be our cause, too__. Because it's not just [African Americans], but really __it's all of us__, who must overcome the __crippling legacy__ of bigotry and injustice. __And we shall overcome__.*

This is an excerpt from Lyndon B. Johnson's "We Shall Overcome" speech. This excerpt uses <u>emotive language</u>. For example, the use of "battle" over a less powerful word like "struggle" makes the issue seem bigger and more important. The phrase "full blessings of American life" evokes patriotic feelings in the listener or reader. Others phrases act to unite the listeners, regardless of race, forcing the listeners to embrace the cause of African Americans as their own. And the use of "crippling legacy" suggests that the bigotry and injustice isn't just bad – it's catastrophic.

> *Tip: While reading, look for examples of repeated words, phrases, or sentence structures; contrast; emotive language; literary elements, such as metaphors or similes; and other word choices that seem very deliberate.*

## HOW TO ANNOTATE

Remember that the essay grader will never see notes made in the test booklet, so there is no reason to fear scribbling notes all over the margins or on the passage. In fact, the more notes there are, the more material there is to draw from while writing the essay.

To annotate a passage:

1. Read the part of the prompt that follows the passage in order to determine the author's primary claim.
2. Underline the author's thesis and topic sentences or supporting arguments.
3. Summarize each argument or paragraph in the margins. The overall structure is easier to see, which helps when analyzing the passage.
4. Underline or circle any specific parts of the passage that may provide a strong quote or paraphrase for the essay.
5. Use the margins to make any notes that might prove helpful when planning and writing the essay.

## PRACTICE WITH ANNOTATING

**Directions:** The following passage is a sample essay passage. We have underlined and summarized the author's thesis and supporting arguments for you. We have also italicized several examples of evidence, reasoning, and stylistic or persuasive elements. For each example, answer the question(s) provided. Then identify 2 additional details to comment on and make your comments in the empty spaces of the margins. Your answers and comments will form the basis for an essay.

As you read the passage below, consider how Paul Bogard uses

- evidence, such as facts or examples, to support claims.
- reasoning to develop ideas and to connect claims and evidence.
- stylistic or persuasive elements, such as word choice or appeals to emotion, to add power to the ideas expressed.

**Adapted from "Let There Be Dark" by Paul Bogard**
*The Los Angeles Times*, December 21, 2012

At my family's cabin on a Minnesota lake, I knew woods so dark that my hands disappeared before my eyes. I knew night skies in which meteors left smoky trails across sugary spreads of stars. But now, **(1)** *when 8 of 10 children born in the United States will never know a sky dark enough for the Milky Way*, I worry we are rapidly losing night's natural darkness before realizing its worth. This winter solstice, as we cheer the days' gradual movement back toward light, let us also remember the irreplaceable value of darkness.

1. Why did the author include this statistic? How does this statistic make the author's arguments seem more urgent?

_____

_____

_____

_____

_____

All life evolved to the steady rhythm of bright days and dark nights. <u>Today, though, when we feel the closeness of nightfall, we reach quickly for a light switch. And too little darkness, meaning too much artificial light at night, spells trouble for all.</u>

**Thesis: Too much light pollution will cause widespread problems.**

**(2)** _Already the World Health Organization classifies working the night shift as a probable human carcinogen, and the American Medical Association has voiced its unanimous support for "light pollution reduction efforts and glare reduction efforts at both the national and state levels."_ **(3)** Our bodies need darkness to produce the hormone melatonin, which keeps certain cancers from developing, and our bodies need darkness for sleep. Sleep disorders have been linked to diabetes, obesity, cardiovascular disease and depression, and recent research suggests one main cause of "short sleep" is "long light." Whether we work at night or simply take our tablets, notebooks and smartphones to bed, there isn't a place for this much artificial light in our lives.

The rest of the world depends on darkness as well, including nocturnal and crepuscular species of birds, insects, mammals, fish and reptiles. Some examples are well known – **(4)** _the 400 species of birds that migrate at night in North America, the sea turtles that come ashore to lay their eggs_ – and some are not, such as _the bats that save American farmers billions in pest control and the moths that pollinate 80% of the world's flora._ Ecological **(5)** _light pollution is like the bulldozer_ of the night, wrecking habitat and disrupting ecosystems several billion years in the making. Simply put, without darkness, Earth's ecology would collapse….

**Supporting Argument: Too little darkness leads to health issues.**

2. How does referencing these two sources make the rest of the information in the paragraph more credible?

_____
_____
_____
_____
_____

3. How do these facts support the argument made in this paragraph?

_____
_____
_____
_____
_____
_____

**Supporting Argument: Too little darkness is bad for the environment.**

4. Why did the author include this information? How does this information make the argument made in this paragraph stronger?

_____
_____
_____
_____
_____

5. How does this simile (comparing light pollution to a bulldozer) help to emphasize the author's opinion of light pollution?

_____
_____
_____
_____
_____
_____

**(6)** _In today's crowded, louder, more fast-paced world, night's darkness can provide solitude, quiet and stillness,_ qualities increasingly in short supply. Every religious tradition has considered darkness invaluable for a soulful life, and the chance to witness the universe has inspired artists, philosophers and everyday stargazers since time began. **(7)** _In a world awash with electric light...how would Van Gogh have given the world his "Starry Night"? Who knows what this vision of the night sky might inspire in each of us, in our children or grandchildren?_

**Supporting Argument: We need darkness for emotional and cultural reasons.**

6.  How does the contrast between "crowded, louder, more fast-paced" and "solitude, quiet and stillness" help to improve the author's argument that darkness has great value?

　　_____
　　_____
　　_____
　　_____
　　_____
　　_____

7.  Why did the author include these rhetorical questions?

　　_____
　　_____
　　_____
　　_____
　　_____
　　_____
　　_____

Yet all over the world, our nights are growing brighter. In the United States and Western Europe, the amount of light in the sky increases an average of about 6% every year. **(8)** _Computer images of the United States at night, based on NASA photographs, show that what was a very dark country as recently as the 1950s is now nearly covered with a blanket of light._ Much of this light is wasted energy, which means wasted dollars. Those of us over 35 are perhaps among the last generation to have known truly dark nights. Even the northern lake where I was lucky to spend my summers has seen its darkness diminish.

**Supporting Argument: Light pollution is getting worse.**

8.  What effect does contrasting the U.S. of today with the U.S. of the 1950s have? Why did the author include this comparison?

　　_____
　　_____
　　_____
　　_____
　　_____
　　_____

**Supporting Argument: This problem can be solved.**

It doesn't have to be this way. Light pollution is readily within our ability to solve, using new lighting technologies and shielding existing lights. Already, many cities and towns across North America and Europe are changing to LED streetlights, which offer dramatic possibilities for controlling wasted light. Other communities are finding success with simply turning off portions of their public lighting after midnight. **(9)** *Even Paris, the famed "city of light," which already turns off its monument lighting after 11 p.m., will this summer start to require its shops, offices and public buildings to turn off lights after 2 a.m.* Though primarily designed to save energy, such reductions in light will also go far in addressing light pollution. But we will never truly address the problem of light pollution until we become aware of the **(10)** *irreplaceable value and beauty of the darkness* we are losing.

9.  Why is Paris, the "city of light," a stronger example than some other city that might have made similar efforts to limit light pollution?

_____

_____

_____

_____

_____

10. Why did the author choose these particular words to describe darkness?

_____

_____

_____

_____

_____

_____

Write an essay in which you explain how Paul Bogard builds an argument to persuade his audience that natural darkness should be preserved. In your essay, analyze how Bogard uses one or more of the features listed above (or features of your own choice) to strengthen the logic and persuasiveness of his argument. Be sure that your analysis focuses on the most relevant features of the passage.

Your essay should not explain whether you agree with Bogard's claims, but rather explain how Bogard builds an argument to persuade his audience.

**Directions:** Read the essay prompt below. While you read the passage, use the lines provided to make notes about the author's use of evidence, reasoning, and other persuasive elements to build his arguments.

As you read the passage below, consider how Katty Kay and Claire Shipman use

- evidence, such as facts or examples, to support claims.
- reasoning to develop ideas and to connect claims and evidence.
- stylistic or persuasive elements, such as word choice or appeals to emotion, to add power to the ideas expressed.

**Adapted from "The Confidence Gap" by Katty Kay and Claire Shipman**
*The Atlantic*, April 14, 2014

In the United States, women now earn more college and graduate degrees than men do. Studies conducted by the likes of Goldman Sachs and Columbia University have found that companies employing women in large numbers outperform their competitors on every measure of profitability. Our competence has never been more obvious. So why are fewer than 5% of Fortune 1000 CEOs female? Why do women make up just 18.5% of Congress? Why do women still, on average, earn 20% less than men?

Some say children change our priorities, and there is truth in this claim. Others point to cultural and institutional barriers to female success. There's truth to that, too. But such explanations are missing something far more basic: Women suffer from an acute lack of confidence. Compared to men, women generally underestimate their abilities.

A 2003 study by David Dunning of Cornell University and Joyce Ehrlinger of Washington State University highlighted the confidence gap among men and women. In the study, male and female college students were given a quiz on scientific reasoning. Before the quiz, the students rated their scientific ability, and after the quiz, they guessed how many questions they had correctly answered. Though male and female students performed about the same on the quiz, female students rated their abilities lower and believed that they had answered fewer questions correctly. To show the real-world impact of self-confidence, the students were invited to participate in a science competition for prizes. Only 49% of female students signed up; 71% of the men participated. "That was a proxy for whether women might seek out certain opportunities," Ehrlinger says. "Because they were less confident in general in their abilities, they did not to want to pursue future opportunities."

Confidence is arguably more important to success than competence. Cameron Anderson, a psychologist who works in the business school at the University of California at Berkeley, has made a career of studying confidence. In 2009, he conducted a series of tests to compare the relative value of confidence and competence. The first test identified overly confident students, those who believed they knew more than they really did, while the second test asked the students to rate one another to assess

how each individual was perceived by the group. The students who were the most overconfident in their abilities achieved the highest standing the group, suggesting that the way others perceive us may have more to do with success than what we are actually capable of.

How we are perceived by others is just one ingredient to success. How we react to different events is another, and a lack of confidence plays a role in this, too. Women have a penchant for assuming the blame when things go wrong, while crediting circumstance or luck for their successes. Women suffer from perfectionism, making us less likely to take risks. These behaviors too often hold women back.

But where does all this come from?

Some research suggests that brain structure could play a role in differences between the ways men and women respond to challenging circumstances. Consider, for example, the fact that women have larger anterior cingulate cortexes, also known as the worrywart center of the brain. Hormones play another role. Women have higher levels of estrogen, which discourages conflict and risk taking. Men have higher levels of testosterone, which encourages a focus on winning and demonstrating power. Thanks to our hormones, we avoid risks while men actively seek them.

These natural tendencies are only further entrenched throughout our schooling. Girls are praised for following the rules and being quiet, while boys are constantly chastised for acting out. As a result, girls learn to keep their heads down while boys learn to let criticism roll off their shoulders. Outside of school, boys learn to relish wins and shrug off losses through athletics. Girls, on the other hand, are far less likely to participate in sports, and those who do are six times more likely to quit than boys, according to the Centers for Disease Control.

So either we were born to a lack of confidence, or we picked it up in childhood. The good news is that a lack of confidence can be fixed. Studies have shown that confidence can be created – if we try something and succeed, we become more confident and more willing to try something new and challenging in the future. If we keep at it, if we force ourselves to take on challenges and face risks, we can make our brains more confidence-prone. What the neuroscientists call *plasticity*, we call *hope*.

---

Write an essay in which you explain how Kay and Shipman build an argument to persuade their audience of the impacts of a confidence gap between men and women. In your essay, analyze how Kay and Shipman use one or more of the features listed above (or features of your own choice) to strengthen the logic and persuasiveness of his argument. Be sure that your analysis focuses on the most relevant features of the passage.

Your essay should not explain whether you agree with Kay and Shipman's claims, but rather explain how Kay and Shipman build an argument to persuade their audience.

## HOMEWORK

**Directions:** Choose one of the essay prompts you annotated in class. You may choose either "Let There Be Dark" of "The Confidence Gap". Using your notes and comments, write an essay on your chosen prompt. Since you are doing this for homework, you will not be timed, but to test your ability to write a good essay under realistic conditions, you should try to limit your writing time to no more than 30 minutes.

## LESSON eB4 – QUOTATIONS AND PARAPHRASING

In this section, we will learn to incorporate evidence and examples from the passage into SAT essays.

### TOPIC OVERVIEW: QUOTATIONS AND PARAPHRASING

In the first lesson of this book, we reviewed grading standards for SAT essays. One of the grading standards reads, "Use of evidence is integrated, comprehensive, relevant, and concrete." To meet this standard, we must accomplish a few key goals:

- Include relevant evidence from the passage in the essay
- Cite that evidence properly
- Incorporate that evidence in a way that thoroughly integrates it into the essay

> *Tip: To score well on the SAT essay, quotes and paraphrases from the passage must be used to support each point made in the essay.*

### WHAT DO WE MEAN BY "EVIDENCE"?

There are two types of evidence involved in an SAT essay: Evidence that the author of the passage uses to support his arguments, and evidence from the passage that is incorporated as support in the essay. When the essay graders look for "use of evidence", they are looking for this second kind of evidence. This evidence might include:

- Specific pieces of evidence (studies, expert testimony, etc.) that the passage author used
- Examples of the author's use of language (word choice, imagery, contrast, repetition, metaphors, etc.)
- The author's logical reasoning

### RELEVANT EVIDENCE

All evidence included in the essay must serve a purpose. Let's look at an example:

> *The author uses several pieces of evidence to support the argument that Americans use vast amounts of harmful chemicals on their lawns. For example, he cites a study that found that Americans spend an estimated $30 billion a year on lawn maintenance.*

In this example, the writer paraphrased a piece of evidence from the provided passage – that's good. Unfortunately, the writer used a piece of evidence that doesn't actually support his claim. Although some portion of the money spent on lawn maintenance likely goes to chemical products, the amount spent on lawn maintenance overall does not at all support the claim that Americans use too many chemicals on their lawns. In fact, we can only assume part of the money goes to purchasing harmful chemicals. This logical disconnect renders the evidence completely irrelevant to the essay writer's main point.

> *Tip: When you reference the passage in your essay, make sure that the segment you are referencing is directly linked to the point that you're trying to make.*

### CITING EVIDENCE

Good writers give credit where credit is due, which is why we should always cite evidence in our essays. Although the essay grader will know that any evidence in the essay came from the passage, we should still practice strong writing techniques by citing our sources. Sometimes this might be as simple as saying, "according to the author…" Other times we might cite the source that the author gave us in the passage. Either way, citing sources displays strong writing skills, which helps essay scores.

### INTEGRATING EVIDENCE

In addition to looking at *whether* evidence from the passage has been incorporated into the essay, the essay graders will look at *how* that evidence is used. Evidence has to logically lead to the point being made in the essay, and it must be smoothly and naturally integrated.

This is where quoting and paraphrasing comes in.

**Quotations** are identical to the original passage and use a narrow segment of the source. For example:

> *To show the benefits of avoiding chemical use, the author contrasts the potentially deadly effects of synthetic fertilizers with the "few weeds and bugs" that would result from avoiding such chemicals.*

In this example, the writer incorporated an exact phrase from the passage. The phrase is used very naturally so that the sentence still flows well, and the quote is only a few words long.

**Paraphrases** are not identical to the passage. When we paraphrase, we put part of the passage into our own words, taking a somewhat broader segment of the source material and condensing it slightly. For example:

> *The author explains that synthetic fertilizers pollute public water sources, causing potentially fatal illnesses.*

In this example, the writer incorporated information from the passage by summarizing it and putting it into his own words.

### WHEN TO QUOTE AND WHEN TO PARAPHRASE

Since the essay is intended to demonstrate strong writing abilities, most of the essay should be in the writer's own words. As a general rule, quotations should be used only when there is a specific reason – otherwise, it is better to rely on paraphrasing.

There are some situations in which it is clearly better to use a direct quote:

- When referencing a quotation from an authority that the author included in the passage
- When analyzing the author's use of specific language
- When the meaning would be lost or altered by rewording something

We use quotations when we need the specific language used in the passage. We use paraphrasing when we want the ideas expressed, and not necessarily the words used to express them.

> *Tip: Only use quotes when you have a specific reason. Most of the time, you should use evidence by paraphrasing.*

## HOW TO USE QUOTATIONS

Incorporating quotations requires a few punctuation rules. Let's review:

- Quotation marks get lonely – always use them in pairs.

- Periods and commas go inside the quotation marks:

  *"Their newest album is too electronic for my taste," Kevin said. "Their old stuff is way better."*

- If a quoted word or phrase fits into the flow of the sentence, a comma is not needed:

  *The phrase "pig-sty" suggests that you don't appreciate the laid back aesthetic of my bedroom.*

- If the quotation follows a dialogue tag (i.e. "he said," "she declared"), a comma is needed:

  *My father always said, "You can only be young once, but you can always be immature."*

- A comma is needed when the quotation follows a dependent clause (a clause that cannot stand on its own):

  *According to Albert Einstein, "Imagination is more important than knowledge."*

- If the quotation follows an independent clause (a clause that could stand as its own sentence) but could be part of the same sentence, use a colon:

  *My history teacher's favorite quote was from Mark Twain: "Never argue with stupid people. They will drag you down to their level and then beat you with experience."*

- A quote within a quote needs special punctuation. Use single quotation marks for quotations within quotations:

  *My teacher sounded incredulous when she asked, "Did you really just say, 'Grammar is dumb'?"*

- A quote that is integrated into the main clause of a sentence (usually introduced by a word like "that" or "because") doesn't generally require a comma:

  *In the article, the author suggests **that** "if we continue to develop artificial intelligence, we may inadvertently replace ourselves as the dominant species."*

  OR

  *The author seems to disagree with the drive to further develop artificial intelligence programs **because** "we may inadvertently replace ourselves as the dominant species."*

### INTEGRATING QUOTES

Correct punctuation is just the first step of properly using quotations. A properly punctuated quote is meaningless without context! The biggest problem with using quotations occurs when a writer assumes that the meaning of the quotation is obvious. Quotations need to be taken from their original context and **fully integrated** into their new home – the essay.

> *Tip: Never assume your reader will read your mind! Every quotation needs to have your own words appear in the same sentence and in surrounding sentences in order to properly incorporate the quote into your essay.*

**Step One:** Introduce the quote rather than simply inserting it into the essay.

*Bad Example:*
*"In an increasingly global – and multilingual – world, can we really afford to remain a nation of monolinguals?" The author is arguing that we should all learn a second language.*

*Good Example:*
*The author argues that we should all learn a second language by asking, "In an increasingly global – and multilingual – world, can we really afford to remain a nation of monolinguals?"*

Both examples establish the same goal, but the second example does a much better job of integrating the quote into the sentence, making the quote feel like a more natural part of the essay.

**Step Two:** Explain what the quotation means. Don't assume the reader already knows.

*Bad example:*
*The author cites a study that "found that individuals who were more proficient in both languages were more resistant than others to the onset of dementia." Other studies found that being bilingual helped babies learn faster.*

*Good example:*
*The author cites a study that "found that individuals who were more proficient in both languages were more resistant than others to the onset of dementia." This suggests that being bilingual has physiological effects that impact not only a person's intelligence, but also their quality of life.*

The first example leaves the reader wondering, "So what?" The quotation has no significant meaning because the essay writer didn't give it any. **A good essay writer will provide meaning for all quotations used in the essay.**

## PRACTICE WITH QUOTES

**Directions:** The following is a transcript of an interview between a reporter and an education reform activist (for the purposes of the assignment, we'll call him Bob Bobson). Pretend that you are the reporter. You are going to write a brief article based on the interview. In your article, you must include *at least four quotes* from the interview. Underline the quotes that you use.

*Reporter:* How did you become involved in education reform?

*Bob Bobson:* I've been a teacher for almost twenty years, and in that time, I've watched our public school systems become increasingly bureaucratic, driven primarily by numbers on a page rather than by a sincere wish for students to succeed. Over time, that emphasis on numbers – on test scores, on dollars, on the number of students receiving school lunch, on every metric you can conceivably measure – has intruded further and further into the classroom, making it harder and harder to focus on each individual student's growth and development. I got tired of watching numbers dictate my classroom, so I decided to do something about it.

*Reporter:* In your opinion, what is the biggest problem in public education today?

*Bob Bobson:* There are so many that I'm not even sure where to begin. Anyone who tells you that there is some magical, silver bullet solution to American education has no idea what they are talking about. The problems in our education system are so complex and interrelated that there is no way to single out just one issue.

*Reporter:* But if you could solve just one problem in today's education system, what would it be?

*Bob Bobson:* I feel that the trajectory of the education system took a turn for the worse with the implementation of test-based policies like No Child Left Behind. Public education certainly was far from perfect long before No Child Left Behind, but that legislation seemed to open the floodgates to standardized testing. Before the era of testing, my students still took standardized tests, but they were more of a tool to provide benchmarks for student progress rather than a measuring stick to determine which students, teachers, and schools failed. Because of the emphasis on standardized tests, teachers can't focus on being teachers. I sometimes feel more like I'm just doing test prep instead of really teaching, drilling my students on facts so they can pass a test instead of helping them to master complex ideas. Getting rid of tests altogether isn't the answer, and reducing the amount of tests or the implications of those tests won't fix American education. But it would allow teachers to actually teach, to focus on the development of their students rather than the test scores of their students.

*Reporter:* So do you think that standardized tests should be eliminated?

*Bob Bobson:* No. I recognize that standardized tests have a role in the education of our children. Though they're far from perfect, they're the only real metric we have to measure student progress. But there's a failure to recognize the imperfection of the metric – these tests have become the end all, be all of student performance. We have to recognize that a test can't measure student progress in its entirety. We have to go back to the time when these tests were a tool for teachers to use instead of a metric to be used against teachers, against struggling students, and against entire schools.

*Use the lines on the following page to write your article. Remember to use at least **four** quotes from the interview and to integrate those quotes into your article!*

## HOW TO PARAPHRASE

Guidelines for properly using paraphrasing in an essay:

- Rephrase the information.
- A paraphrase must be accurate and must include the whole idea of the original author.
- The information being paraphrased should be integrated into the essay.
- Paraphrase whenever possible. Only use quotes when the author's specific language is important.
- As with quotes, always explain the significance of the information being paraphrased.

Let's look at an example:

> *Original source material: "The collective evidence from a number of similar studies suggests that bilingual abilities improve the brain's executive function, the command system that controls the processes for planning, problem solving, and performing several other mentally demanding tasks."*

> *Example of Bad Paraphrasing:*
> *According to the author, a number of studies show that bilingual abilities improve the brain's executive function, which is the command system that controls mentally demanding tasks.*

> *Example of Good Paraphrasing:*
> *According to the author, there are several studies that support the idea that bilingual abilities may translate into heightened executive function, meaning that bilinguals may be better at mentally demanding tasks like problem solving.*

The example of bad paraphrasing borrows much of its wording from the original source. In fact, nearly every word in this example can be found in the original quote. The example of good paraphrasing, on the other hand, not only properly rephrases the information in the original quote, but also helps to clarify the significance of the information by better explaining what improving the brain's executive function really means.

## INTEGRATING PARAPHRASES

As with quotations, the paraphrased information has to be integrated into the essay, and the information being paraphrased should be properly explained. Let's use the same example to explore this idea:

> *Poorly Integrated Paraphrasing:*
> *According to the author, there are several studies that support the idea that bilingual abilities may translate into heightened executive function, meaning that bilinguals may be better at mentally demanding tasks like problem solving. This supports the idea that bilinguals are smarter than monolinguals.*

The essay writer paraphrased information from the passage, but then he made a big logical leap that fails to provide adequate reasoning to give the paraphrased information a good home.

> *Properly Integrated Paraphrasing:*
> *According to the author, there are several studies that support the idea that bilingual abilities may translate into heightened executive function, meaning that bilinguals may be better at mentally demanding tasks like problem solving. In establishing that bilingual abilities affect areas of the brain far beyond language skills, the author is further supporting the idea that bilinguals may in fact be smarter than monolinguals.*

This example uses the exact same paraphrased information, but it more effectively integrates the information by better linking the information to the conclusion that bilinguals may be smarter than monolinguals.

## PRACTICE WITH QUOTING AND PARAPHRASING

**Directions:** For each of the following paragraphs, use one quote and one paraphrase to evaluate the author's main argument. The first one has been done for you as an example. Note that the examples follow the rules of the lesson: A quotation must be word for word and should be used when the language is as important as the content; a paraphrase must be accurate and in your own words; and both quotations and paraphrases must be explained in your own words.

1. Agave nectar was lauded as a natural and healthy alternative to the "evil" high-fructose corn syrup that is ubiquitous in our food supply, but it turns out that "natural" and "healthy" aren't necessarily synonymous. High-fructose corn syrup suffers from a rather misleading name in that the fructose content is only high relative to regular old corn syrup. High-fructose corn syrup has fructose content similar to that of table sugar – between 50 and 55%. Agave nectar, on the other hand, is 90% fructose, a fact that was widely overlooked when agave began being marketed as a natural alternative to the laboratory evils of high-fructose corn syrup.

   **Quoting the source:** The author points out that agave nectar's high fructose content "was widely overlooked when agave began being marketed as a natural alternative to the laboratory evils of high-fructose corn syrup." In contrasting "natural" and "laboratory evils", the author is using deliberate word choices to further support the argument that natural ingredients aren't necessarily healthier than man-made ingredients.

   **Paraphrasing the source:** According to the author, although agave nectar was celebrated as a natural and healthy sweetener, it actually has a far higher fructose content than high-fructose corn syrup. By establishing the relative fructose contents of each sweetener, the author is able to provide an objective metric that proves that natural ingredients aren't necessarily healthy.

2. Hot-button national issues most often arise due to the actions of lobbyists, political action committees, or well-funded think tanks, which is one of the things that makes the issue of labelling foods containing genetically modified organisms (GMOs) unique: This particular national movement stems almost entirely from constituents rather than big, politically motivated groups. In state after state where GMO labeling has been proposed, the politicians pushing it tell the same story. The issue, they say, was hardly on their radar until a massive amount of constituent pressure put it there. Vermont state senator Bobby Starr found himself bombarded by constituents demanding GMO labeling. Everywhere he went, everyone from villagers at their annual town meeting to children at a school assembly seemed to want to talk about GMOs in their food. As a result of constituent pressure, Starr signed on as a supporter of a GMO-labelling bill that made Vermont the first state to require labeling.

   **Quoting the source:**

   _____
   _____
   _____
   _____
   _____

   **Paraphrasing the source:**

   _____
   _____
   _____
   _____
   _____

3. With the cost of prisons exceeding $60 billion a year, state and local governments have an obligation to create policies that reduce recidivism rates, ensuring that newly released prisoners stay out of jail instead of coming back in through a revolving door. North Carolina, for example, found that probation violations accounted for

half of those sent to prison each year. Three-quarters of probation violators who were sent to prison had not committed any other offenses – they had simply missed a meeting with a probation officer or been in the wrong place at the wrong time, crimes that became punishable by lengthy prison sentences. By relaxing rules for probation offenses and providing better transitional services to recently released inmates, North Carolina was able to reduce its recidivism rate by nearly 20% in just three years. As a result, the state was able to close down nine correctional facilities, freeing up the money to hire more probation officers and lend more support to social services that help keep former inmates from returning to jail.

**Quoting the source:**

_____
_____
_____
_____
_____

**Paraphrasing the source:**

_____
_____
_____
_____
_____

4.   Interestingly, there is no clear consensus on the traits necessary for success. Though most people believe that things like intelligence, competence, and motivation are the primary ingredients, several studies show that an individual's level of success may rest on far more superficial traits. In fact, one study by professors at Duke's Fuqua School of Business suggests that an individual's appearance may be a deciding factor. In the study, 2,000 people were asked to look at a long series of photos. Some showed CEOs and others showed nonexecutives, but the participants did not know who was who. Participants were asked to rate the subjects based on how "competent" they looked – a superficial judgment, to be sure. Surprisingly, participants overwhelmingly identified the CEOs as more competent looking. More surprisingly, the more competent a CEO looked, the bigger the paycheck he or she received in real life. And yet the authors found no relationship whatsoever between how competent a CEO looked and the financial performance of his or her company, suggesting that it is the appearance of competence that matters more than the actual presence of competence.

**Quoting the source:**

_____
_____
_____
_____
_____

**Paraphrasing the source:**

_____
_____
_____
_____
_____

**HOMEWORK**

**Directions:** Read the essay prompt below. While you read the passage, use the lines provided to make notes about the author's use of evidence, reasoning, and other persuasive elements to build his arguments. You will use these notes to write an essay on the passage. Since you're doing this at home, you won't be timed, but you should try to limit yourself to just 50 minutes to read and analyze the passage and to write your essay.

As you read the passage below, consider how David Leonhardt uses

- evidence, such as facts or examples, to support claims.
- reasoning to develop ideas and to connect claims and evidence.
- stylistic or persuasive elements, such as word choice or appeals to emotion, to add power to the ideas expressed.

**Adapted from "The Reality of Student Debt" by David Leonhardt**
*The New York Times*, **June 24, 2014**

With total student loan debt past the $1 trillion mark, it isn't difficult to find tales of woe surrounding young graduates. We are barraged with stories of baristas, cashiers, or freelancers holding college degrees that they can't use and saddled with tens of thousands of dollars of student loans they can't pay.

Such anecdotes have created the impression that massive levels of debt are typical for college students. They're not. Only 7% of young-adult households have education debt of more than $50,000. By contrast, 58% of such households have less than $10,000 in education debt. This national focus on what is really an atypical problem masks much more problematic education issues, ranging from a college dropout crisis to a lack of adequate preparation in our public schools.

Despite the media spin, higher education's worst victims are not the graduates of expensive colleges struggling to pay loans while underemployed. The vastly bigger problem is the hundreds of thousands of people who leave college with modest student debt and no degree. These students take on student debt, but do not see a significant increase in income as a result of their time in college. In a cost-benefit analysis, these students get only the cost.

According to a recent report by the Brookings Institution, "Among households with some college but no bachelor's degree, the incidence of debt increased from 11 to 41 percent." This is hardly surprising given the growing number of college students who fail to earn a degree. A 2011 Harvard Graduate School of Education study found that only 56% of students who enter four-year programs graduate within six years. That number plummets to just 22% for for-profit colleges.

The college dropout crisis is, in and of itself, a symptom of another issue: a lack of college preparation at the high school level. According to ACT, only 25% of test takers are proficient in English, math, reading, and

science. Worse yet, more than 25% of test takers failed to demonstrate proficiency in even a single subject.

While many may argue that a single test, such as the ACT, cannot possibly measure something as nebulous as college-preparedness, there are plenty of other numbers to support ACT's findings. For example, one in five college students are required to enroll in remedial courses before being allowed to take credit-bearing courses. This creates a situation in which underprepared students must borrow large amounts of money to take college courses that don't confer credit towards a degree, all because their high schools failed to teach them the basic knowledge and skills necessary for college success. This might be acceptable if such students ultimately earned a degree that resulted in higher earnings in order to pay off that debt, but students who are required to take remedial courses are up to three times more likely than other students to drop out before completing a degree.

College professors agree that their students are poorly prepared for the rigors of college. A study by the *Chronicle of Higher Education* found that 90% of professors judge their students to be "not very well prepared" for college level reading, writing, and researching. Today's college students have difficulty writing within the constraints of standard conventions, crafting logical arguments, and identifying and citing sources. At DePaul University, for example, a student's paper included several paragraphs in purple text; the paragraphs had been copied and pasted directly from a website. When confronted, the student was not defensive – he just wanted to know how to change the text from purple to black. Such cases are sadly typical; surveys from 2006 to 2010 by Donald L. McCabe, a business professor at Rutgers University, found that about 40% of undergraduates admitted to plagiarism in their papers.

Clearly the problem of student debt is merely the tip of the iceberg. Beneath that issue lies a host of broader education problems, from college preparation in high school to the prevalence of remedial education in college to a lack of support for those students most likely to leave college without a degree. Yes, it is terrible that college tuition has risen at a rate that far outpaces inflation. Yes, it is terrible that lenders allow students to borrow far more money than they can reasonably pay back. But the fact that so many student debtors never earn a degree to justify their debt is arguably a much greater issue.

---

Write an essay in which you explain how Leonhardt builds an argument to persuade his audience that the student debt crisis masks broader education issues. In your essay, analyze how Leonhardt uses one or more of the features listed above (or features of your own choice) to strengthen the logic and persuasiveness of his argument. Be sure that your analysis focuses on the most relevant features of the passage.

Your essay should not explain whether you agree with Leonhardt's claims, but rather explain how Leonhardt builds an argument to persuade his audience.

## LESSON eB5 – EVALUATING LANGUAGE

In this section, we will learn to evaluate an author's use of language to persuade an audience.

### TOPIC OVERVIEW: EVALUATING LANGUAGE

Every SAT essay prompt will include these instructions: "As you read the passage below, consider how [the author] uses stylistic or persuasive elements, *such as word choice or appeals to emotion*, to add power to the ideas expressed."

Looking at the author's evidence and reasoning isn't enough –we also need to evaluate the author's use of language.

Why does language matter so much? Persuasion requires more than just facts. Yes, facts can be used to persuade an audience, but if an argument consists of nothing but facts, it may as well be an excerpt from a text book. For persuasive writing to be truly persuasive, it must not only utilize strong evidence, but also incorporate powerful language choices.

Before we begin, let's preview some of the concepts of persuasive language.

## PERSUASIVE LANGUAGE PREVIEW

**Directions:** Each pair of arguments takes the same stance on a given issue. For each pair, circle the letter for the argument that you believe is more persuasive. Then use the lines provided to explain your choice. Since the arguments themselves are fairly similar, pay close attention to the language the author of each argument uses.

1.  A) When educational leaders decided to create specialized magnet schools, they didn't just get it wrong, they got it backwards. They pulled the best and brightest students from our communities and sent them away. The students who were once in the middle of the class now find themselves in an environment where the peers who have the greatest influence in their school are the least positive role models.

    B) The selective admission requirements at top magnet schools result in a student body comprised primarily of students who have had access to academic opportunities like private tutoring. As a result, magnet schools have become bastions of the upper-middle class, leaving the surrounding public schools with an imbalanced proportion of impoverished students and a lack of adequate funding.

    Why did you choose this argument?

    _____

    _____

    _____

2.  A) Noncompete agreements, a common tool used by employers to prevent the disclosure of proprietary information, may in fact be detrimental to innovation. A growing body of evidence suggests that innovation, productivity, and economic growth are all greater in regions in which local laws prohibit such contracts – most notably, Silicon Valley, the hub of the nation's technology industry.

    B) Noncompete agreements may help employers retain employees, but are they worth the cost? The employees retained by noncompete agreements remain with their employers not out of loyalty or drive, but because they have no other options. Workers who are not motivated create companies that lack innovation and productivity. If noncompete agreements create unhappy workers and unproductive companies, why are they such a common feature in modern employment agreements?

    Why did you choose this argument?

    _____

    _____

    _____

3.   A) Across America, the ranks of the working poor are growing. Low-paying industries such as retail and food preparation have generated 44% of jobs added since the Great Recession. These jobs tend to pay minimum wage and offer few benefits, leaving such workers struggling to make ends meet. The Congressional Budget Office has estimated that raising the national minimum wage from $7.25 to $10.10 would lift 900,000 people out of poverty, allowing hundreds of thousands of families to escape the shadow of fear and shame that life under the poverty line creates.

     B) Although low-paying industries such as retail and food preparation accounted for 22% of the jobs lost in the Great Recession, those same industries are responsible for 44% of the jobs added since then. Because low-wage workers now make up such a large share of the workforce, an increase to the national minimum wage would have greater impact today than in decades past. In fact, the Congressional Budget Office estimates that an increase from $7.25 to $10.10 would raise 900,000 people above the poverty line.

     Why did you choose this argument?

     _____

     _____

     _____

### EVALUATING PERSUASIVE LANGUAGE

Let's start by looking at the examples of persuasive language that we just reviewed. These examples provide a glimpse at a handful of persuasive language techniques.

*Example 1*

Both A and B argue that magnet schools degrade the quality of surrounding public schools, but they do so in different ways. Argument A uses *emotive language* to emphasize the effects magnet schools have on students who remain at surrounding public schools, while argument B uses formal language to make a more economic-based argument. Both are persuasive, but A uses emotion while B relies exclusively on logic.

*Example 2*

Both A and B argue that noncompete agreements create more harm than good. Argument A relies primarily on evidence and logic, using high-level formal language to make a clear case. Argument B uses less formal language and relies on a pair of *rhetorical questions* to emphasize the idea that noncompete agreements harm both workers and employers.

*Example 3*

Both A and B use statistical evidence to support the argument that raising the minimum wage would reduce poverty. Argument A uses phrases such as "working poor," "struggling to make ends meet," and "escape the shadow of fear and shame" to create a more *emotional argument*. Argument B relies almost exclusively on statistics to create an objective argument.

*What do these examples show us?*

In each example, the authors make very similar arguments. One argument isn't necessarily better than another, but the language choices the authors make can impact the ways in which arguments persuade a reader. When writing SAT essays, we need to evaluate how an author's use of language alters his or her arguments.

## Persuasive Language Techniques

We've listed some of the most common persuasive language techniques in the chart below. Mastering the terminology in this chart can help to create stronger SAT essays by allowing us to better evaluate an author's use of persuasive language techniques.

> *Tip: This chart is a cheat sheet to help evaluate language in a passage. Keep it handy during practice essays so that these terms become familiar!*

| Technique | Examples | Persuasive Effect |
|---|---|---|
| **Language Style**<br><br>The kind of language used to suit the writer's purpose, such as formal, informal, colloquial, informative, and so on. | *Formal:* "If we consider the situation in emergency departments, which are experiencing increasingly low staff retention rates, there are concerns about the capacity of hospitals to maintain adequate doctor to patient ratios."<br><br>*Colloquial:* "Emergency department staff are quitting left and right, leading to a situation in which an emergency room visit might last for days because of a shortage of doctors." | Language style is deliberately chosen to influence the reader. In general, an author's language can often be described as either formal or informal/colloquial.<br><br>*Formal* language creates an impression of authority that can impress readers with the author's knowledge.<br><br>*Informal* or *Colloquial* language is accessible and familiar, which can make readers believe that the author is on the same wavelength as them. |
| **Inclusive/Exclusive Language**<br><br>Inclusive language includes "we," "our," or "us," while exclusive language includes "them" or "their." | *Inclusive:* "We must act to improve student outcomes for the good of the nation's future."<br><br>*Exclusive:* "Educators have a responsibility to improve student outcomes. If they don't act, the nation's future is at risk." | *Inclusive* language can suggest that the author is part of a group, or it can be used to include the reader in the argument, making the reader more likely to agree.<br><br>*Exclusive* language is often used to create a divide or to persuade the reader that some other party is responsible for a problem. |
| **Emotive Language**<br><br>The deliberate use of emotive words to play on the readers' feelings and create an emotional appeal. | "The governor has faced several ethics complaints." *vs.* "The governor is just another sleazy, corrupt politician."<br><br>The second example uses emotive language to encourage the reader to become angry about the governor's ethics scandals. | Emotive language evokes a strong emotional response in order to manipulate the reader's opinions. |
| **Connotations**<br><br>Connotations are implied meanings of words. They create subtle differences between similar words. | Consider the word "thin." There are lots of words with similar meanings (slender, lithe, slim, skinny, lean, lanky, wasted, gangly, spindly). Most people would prefer to be described as "slender" or "slim" rather than "wasted" or "gangly" because of the positive and negative connotations of these words. | Authors carefully select words for the impact the words may have on a reader.<br><br>Connotations can also be used to create an emotional response in the reader. |

| Technique | Examples | Persuasive Effect |
|---|---|---|
| **Figurative Language**<br><br>Time to dust off those literary terms! Figurative language includes similes, metaphors, imagery, and hyperbole.<br><br>• **Similes**: Comparing two things using "like" or "as"<br>• **Metaphors**: Comparing two things without using "like" or "as"<br>• **Imagery**: Colorful language to create strong descriptions<br>• **Hyperbole**: Exaggeration | *Simile:* "Citizenship was thrown around like confetti." Suggests that those who granted citizenship so freely devalued citizenship.<br>*Metaphor:* "America is a melting pot of cultures." More emotionally appealing than saying "America is a multi-cultural nation."<br>*Imagery:* "After the battle, bodies were stacked four deep, and the buzz of gluttonous flies was inescapable." More emotionally evocative than "The battle resulted in many casualties."<br>*Hyperbole:* "Every weekend, the city is overrun by beggars." "Overrun" suggests that the city is literally filled with beggars, which is an exaggeration used to emphasize the point that the number of beggars increases on the weekends. | *Similes* are often used to make a point using more colorful language.<br><br>*Metaphors* are often used to evoke emotional responses.<br><br>*Imagery* can be used to engage the reader or to appeal to the reader's emotions.<br><br>*Hyperbole* is often used to emphasize a point, to mock opposing opinions, or to instill fear in the reader by exaggerating the worst possible outcome. |
| **Repetition**<br><br>Repeated words, phrases, sentence patterns, or ideas | "We shall go on to the end, we shall fight in France…we shall defend our Island, whatever the cost may be, we shall fight on the beaches, we shall fight on the landing grounds, we shall fight in the fields and in the streets…we shall never surrender." In his famous "Blood, Sweat, and Tears" speech, Winston Churchill used repetition to encourage his listeners to support British troops in World War II. | By repeating words, phrases, sentence patterns, or ideas, the author can reinforce an argument and make it more memorable. |
| **Rhetorical Questions**<br><br>Questions that do not require an answer and are asked for effect only. | "Do we want our children to grow up in a world where they are threatened with violence on every street corner?" | Rhetorical questions engage the audience and encourage readers to consider the issue and accept the author's argument. Alternatively, these questions can be used to suggest that the answer to the question is so obvious that anyone who disagrees is foolish. |
| **Humor**<br><br>Puns, sarcasm, irony, satire, or jokes | "The controversial new exhibit at the Museum of Modern Art has many visitors totally *artraged*." The use of the pun (artraged as a play on outraged) downplays the visitors' outrage. | Humor can be persuasive by dismissing opposing views, providing a more engaging and friendly tone, or swaying an audience by letting them in on the joke. |

## PRACTICE WITH PERSUASIVE LANGUAGE

**Directions:** Each of the following paragraphs is from an essay passage called "Why Mow? The Case Against Lawns," in which the author, Michael Pollan, argues that Americans' pristine lawns are creating health and environmental hazards. For each paragraph, write 3-5 sentences in which you analyze the author's use of language. Circle any terms that you draw from the Persuasive Language Techniques chart.

1. Like the interstate highway system, like fast-food chains, like television, the lawn has served to unify the American landscape; it is what makes the suburbs of Cleveland and Tucson look more alike than not. France has its formal, geometric gardens, England its picturesque parks, and America this unbounded democratic river of manicured lawn along which we array our houses.

   _____

   _____

   _____

   _____

   _____

   _____

2. Americans did not invent the lawn; lawns had been popular in England since Tudor times. But in England, lawns were usually found only on estates; the Americans democratized them, cutting the vast manorial greenswards into quarter-acre slices everyone could afford. The American lawn is an egalitarian conceit, implying that there is no reason to hide behind fence or hedge since we all occupy the same middle class.

   _____

   _____

   _____

   _____

   _____

   _____

3. However democratic a lawn may be with respect to one's neighbors, with respect to nature it is authoritarian. Under the mower's brutal indiscriminate rotor, the landscape is subdued, homogenized, dominated utterly. We superimpose our lawns on the land. And since the geography and climate of much of this country is poorly suited to turfgrasses (none of which are native), this can't be accomplished without the tools of 20th-century industrial civilization, with its chemical fertilizers, pesticides, herbicides, and machinery.

   _____

   _____

   _____

   _____

   _____

_____

_____

4.  Lately we have begun to recognize that we are poisoning ourselves with our lawns, which receive, on average, more pesticide and herbicide per acre than any crop grown in this country. According to the EPA, 3 million tons of synthetic fertilizer and over 30,000 tons of pesticides are dumped on our lawns each year.

_____

_____

_____

_____

_____

_____

5.  If we are to maintain our democratic lawn, we must accept a degree of imperfection. The national obsession with the picture-perfect, weed- and pest-free carpet of lush, green grass has led to overuse of damaging chemicals, and weaning ourselves off of these chemicals will require that we live with a few weeds and bugs.

_____

_____

_____

_____

_____

_____

_____

6.  Should we prove unable to live with imperfect lawns, we may soon need to live without healthy lakes, rivers, and streams. We may need to live without venturing out of doors, since contact with chemical fertilizers and pesticides can be dangerous to our health. We may need to avoid using public water supplies. But at least we would have the comfort of knowing that our green space is immaculate, the envy of all the neighbors.

_____

_____

_____

_____

_____

_____

_____

_____

## HOMEWORK

**Directions:** This essay prompt features many examples of persuasive language techniques. As you read the passage, use the lines provided to make notes about the author's persuasive techniques, including use of evidence, reasoning, and language. You will use these notes to write an essay on the passage. Since you're doing this at home, you won't be timed, but you should try to limit yourself to just 50 minutes to read and analyze the passage and to write your essay.

As you read the passage below, consider how Sherry Turkle uses

- evidence, such as facts or examples, to support claims.
- reasoning to develop ideas and to connect claims and evidence.
- stylistic or persuasive elements, such as word choice or appeals to emotion, to add power to the ideas expressed.

**Adapted from "The Flight from Conversation" by Sherry Turkle**
*The New York Times*, **April 22, 2012**

We inhabit a technological universe in which we are always communicating, yet we have sacrificed conversation for mere connection. At home, families spend time together by spending time apart, texting or reading emails. At work, executives text during board meetings. We stare at our phones during classes and on dates.

Over the past 15 years, I've studied technologies of mobile connection and talked to hundreds of people of all backgrounds about their techno-centric lives. I've learned that the devices we cling to are so powerful that they change not only what we do but who we are.

Thanks to the ubiquity of smart phones, we've become accustomed to a new notion of togetherness. We are now able to be with one another, and also elsewhere, connected to wherever we want to be. We want control over where we focus our attention, and modern technology has given this to us. As a result, we can end up hiding from one another, even as we are constantly connected to one another.

Walking through a college library, an office space, or even a crowded street, one sees the same thing: we are together, but each of us is in our own bubble, furiously connected to keyboards and touchscreens. A senior partner at a Boston law firm described just this when asked about the atmosphere in his offices. Each morning, young associates spread an array of technologies across their desks: laptops, iPods, and cell phones. They put on their massive, noise-cancelling headphones and get to work. The office is quiet, but the silence has an unhealthy feel. In this quiet, there is no exchange of ideas, no building of interpersonal relationships. In this quiet, the law firm cannot be a team because each player is disparate, plugged in and tuned out.

In the silence of connection, we are comforted by being in touch with many people while controlling just how close those people can get. Texting, e-mailing, and posting allow us to present the self we want to be. We can edit and, if we wish to, delete. We can be the cleanest and most perfect version of ourselves. Human relationships are messy and demanding; technology allows us to clean them up. But in the process, we shortchange ourselves, eliminating the glorious chaos of human emotion. The move from conversation to connection is part of this, and over time we may forget that there is a difference.

We are tempted to believe that our tiny doses of online connection add up to a greater conversation, but they don't. Connecting in doses may work for gathering discrete bits of information, but it doesn't allow us to understand and know one another. In conversation, we tend to each other. We pay attention to tone and nuance. We are called upon to see things from another's point of view.

By contrast, these constant connections allow us to focus entirely on ourselves and our desire to be heard. Because these devices allow us the illusion that we will always be heard, we never have to be alone. Indeed, being alone is now a problem that can be solved. When people are alone, even for a few moments, they fidget and reach for a device. Here, connection works like a symptom, not a cure, and our constant impulse to connect shapes a new way of being. No longer able to appreciate solitude, we turn to other people, but through the shield of a device, we don't experience them as they are.

Even when we do interact face to face, the mere omnipresence of our devices harms interaction. A recent study at the University of Essex showed that simply having a phone nearby can be detrimental to our attempts at interpersonal connection. Participants in the study reported feeling less trust and thought that their partners showed less empathy if there was a cell phone present during the pair's conversations. In other words, even when we strive for meaningful relationships through conversation rather than connectivity, our devices may interfere.

We think constant connection will make us feel less lonely. The opposite is true. If we are unable to be alone, we are far more likely to be lonely. After all, how can we ever hope to truly enjoy the company of others if we can no longer stand the company of ourselves?

---

Write an essay in which you explain how Turkle builds an argument to persuade her audience that the constant presence of smart phones and other devices has altered our interactions for the worse. In your essay, analyze how Turkle uses one or more of the features listed above (or features of your own choice) to strengthen the logic and persuasiveness of her argument. Be sure that your analysis focuses on the most relevant features of the passage.

Your essay should not explain whether you agree with Turkle's claims, but rather explain how Turkle builds an argument to persuade her audience.

## LESSON EB6 – DEVELOPING A THESIS

In this section, we will focus on developing and supporting a thesis statement throughout your essay.

### TOPIC OVERVIEW: DEVELOPING A THESIS

It's fairly easy to create a thesis statement for a persuasive essay because we have to state a claim. However, creating a thesis statement for an analytical essay, like the one on the SAT, can be more difficult.

An analytical essay answers *how* something does what it does – in this case, how the author builds an argument. Thus the thesis statement will answer the question, "How does the author of the passage build his/her arguments?" A good SAT thesis statement should:

- be specific.
- cover only what will be discussed in the essay.
- appear in the first paragraph.

Remember that one of the grading standards for an SAT essay is that the "central claim is clearly stated, focused, and strongly maintained." The thesis states the central claim, so a good thesis is vital in order to meet that grading standard.

### STRONG VS. WEAK THESIS STATEMENTS

A strong thesis statement provides the readers with a clearly focused lens through which to view the arguments in the passage.

> *Example: Throughout the article, Smith relies on empirical studies paired with a formal writing style in order to better support his arguments by establishing his authority in the field of social psychology.*

This example offers a thesis statement that clearly identifies the tools that the author used to build his arguments – studies and a formal writing style. From this thesis, we know that the essay is going to discuss Smith's use of studies and formal writing, thus giving us a glimpse of the rest of the essay.

A weak thesis statement gives the readers a fuzzy lens that does not help them to better understand how the author built his/her arguments.

> *Example: Smith creates strong arguments with his evidence and writing style.*

This example is much less specific than the first one. Although it identifies two things that the essay will discuss – evidence and writing style – it fails to clarify exactly what kind of evidence or writing style will be discussed, nor does it explain how those two things helped to make the author's arguments stronger.

> *Tip: Don't forget – A strong thesis is clear and focused. A weak thesis is vague and fuzzy.*

## EVALUATING THESIS STATEMENTS

**Directions**: For this exercise, pretend you are helping a friend write better thesis statements. For each of the following sample thesis statements, determine whether the thesis is "strong" or "weak." Use the lines provided to explain why you think each statement is strong or weak.

1. Smith makes his arguments stronger by incorporating a lot of evidence.

    **WEAK**                    **STRONG**

    _____

    _____

2. Throughout the article, Smith relies on statistical evidence to bolster his arguments.

    **WEAK**                    **STRONG**

    _____

    _____

3. By pairing informal language with emotional appeals, Smith encourages his audience to agree with his arguments in spite of their relative lack of concrete evidence.

    **WEAK**                    **STRONG**

    _____

    _____

4. Smith's use of language makes his arguments stronger despite a lack of real evidence supporting them.

    **WEAK**                    **STRONG**

    _____

    _____

5. Smith's lack of evidence can be overlooked because his use of language engages the reader.

    **WEAK**                    **STRONG**

    _____

    _____

6. Smith's unique combination of colloquial language and statistical evidence results in surprisingly strong arguments that are further supported by Smith's background as an expert in the field.

   **WEAK**                    **STRONG**

   _____

   _____

7. Throughout the article, Smith incorporates a variety of persuasive techniques, including emotional appeals, empirical evidence, and an engaging writing style, in order to convince his readers that his seemingly impossible conclusion is, in fact, completely plausible.

   **WEAK**                    **STRONG**

   _____

   _____

8. At various points throughout the article, Smith utilizes a variety of persuasive techniques like persuasive language and evidence to thoroughly support his arguments, resulting in a very persuasive article that thoroughly convinces readers to agree with Smith's main claim.

   **WEAK**                    **STRONG**

   _____

   _____

9. Because of his use of evidence, Smith's arguments are very strong.

   **WEAK**                    **STRONG**

   _____

   _____

10. Smith explores the entire spectrum of persuasive techniques, including use of persuasive language, incorporation of empirical evidence and expert testimony, and appeals both the reader's logic and emotions.

    **WEAK**                    **STRONG**

    _____

    _____

**THESIS STATEMENT RECIPE**

The chart below offers several examples of each of the ingredients for a strong thesis statement. For each ingredient, use the empty space in the "Examples" column to come up with at least two more examples.

| Ingredient | Purpose | Examples |
|---|---|---|
| Introductory phrase | Gives context to the thesis statement | • Throughout the article,<br>• At various points in "Article Title," |
| Author's action | Uses formal language to establish the subject and verb of the thesis statement | • [Author's name] uses…<br>• [Author's name] relies on… |
| Persuasive elements | Introduces the specific persuasive elements that you're going to discuss in your essay | • Formal language<br>• Emotional appeals<br>• A variety of empirical evidence |
| Effect of persuasive elements | Specifies *how* these elements make the author's arguments stronger | • In order to establish his authority in the field.<br>• In order to persuade the reader to agree with his claims in spite of their relative lack of concrete evidence. |

*Putting it together:*

Introductory Phrase: Throughout the article,
Author's Action: Gioia incorporates
Persuasive Elements: a variety of concrete evidence that is presented using artful and emotive language
Effect of Persuasive Elements: in order to appeal to both the reader's logic and emotions.

**Final Thesis:** Throughout the article, Gioia incorporates a variety of concrete evidence that is presented using artful and emotive language in order to appeal to both the reader's logic and emotions.

## THESIS STATEMENT PRACTICE

**Directions**: Each of the following blurbs summarizes a potential essay prompt passage. For each blurb, use the ingredients of a good thesis statement to build a potential thesis. Don't worry about whether your thesis statement is accurate to the prompt passage – just focus on using the ingredients to form a clear and specific thesis.

1. **Passage Title**: "Cursive in a Modern World"
   **Author's Name**: E.L. Harper
   **Author's Main Claim**: Schools across the nation are dropping cursive handwriting in their curricula, but cursive has an important role that extends far beyond mere handwriting.
   **Supporting Arguments**: Learning cursive affects neurological development by improving fine motor skills and language acquisition; replacing learning cursive with learning to type is insufficient as typing does not build similar neurological pathways; if future scholars cannot read cursive handwriting, many historical documents will become all but meaningless since nearly all archival documents are handwritten in cursive.
   **Persuasive Elements Included in Passage**: Several neurological studies, expert testimony, emotional appeals

   Potential Thesis Statement: _____

   _____

   _____

2. **Passage Title**: "Higher Education for All?"
   **Author's Name**: Jonathan Fields
   **Author's Main Claim**: Requiring students who lack the skills, resources, or motivation for college to pursue college readiness fails to improve outcomes for both college-bound and non-college-bound students.
   **Supporting Arguments**: Some students simply will not, and probably should not, go to college; requiring college-readiness for all students decreases academic performance and increases dropout rates for those students who will not go to college; focusing on college-readiness for non-college-bound students diverts resources away from those students who are likely to go to college; providing career training for non-college-bound students greatly improves outcomes for those students
   **Persuasive Elements Included in Passage**: Humor, statistical evidence, logical reasoning

   Potential Thesis Statement: _____

   _____

   _____

3. **Passage Title**: "The Root of Our Problems"
   **Author's Name**: Elizabeth Ross
   **Author's Main Claim**: Ameliorating poverty would solve many societal ills, including high crime rates, poor educational outcomes, and budget shortfalls that result in bad infrastructure and cuts to services.
   **Supporting Arguments**: Poverty is the root of most common problems in cities; high crime rates, which result in high incarceration rates and high corrections costs, are the direct result of widespread poverty; widespread poverty is the biggest factor contributing to poor educational outcomes; the costs of poverty strain city budgets and result in cuts to things like infrastructure maintenance and resident services.
   **Persuasive Elements Included in Passage**: Expert testimony, statistical evidence, emotional appeals

   Potential Thesis Statement: _____

   _____

   _____

## MORE THESIS TIPS AND STRATEGIES

Here are some additional tips and strategies for strong thesis statements:

*One sentence or two?*
No one wrote a rule anywhere that says that a proper thesis statement can't have more than one sentence, but since a thesis statement should always be concise, it's better to utilize one-sentence thesis statements – especially on the SAT essay, where the reader will only have a few short minutes to score the essay.

*How much is enough?*
In any given passage, we could probably identify at least three or four – if not ten – persuasive strategies. <u>It will not be possible to incorporate all of these in a timed essay and still score well.</u> Since the essay is timed, and since part of the grading standards evaluate the clarity and focus of the essay, it's better choose just two – maybe three – techniques to write about. <u>Those are the only techniques that should be included in the thesis statement.</u>

*Is the thesis enough, or should there be a full introduction?*
It's important to provide context for the thesis by including a well-developed introduction. The introductory paragraph should be brief, but it should also contain some important information:

- The author's name and the name of the article
- The author's main claim and/or purpose
- The thesis statement

Of course the reader already knows the purpose of the essay and what the passage is about – but it's still a good idea to provide some context for the thesis rather than just jumping into the essay.

> *Example:*
>
> *In "Why Literature Matters," author Dana Gioia argues that a declining interest in reading, particularly among American youth, could have far-reaching consequences that extend well beyond the realm of literature, ending with an appeal to the reader to prevent such terrible consequences from occurring. Throughout the article, Gioia incorporates a variety of concrete evidence that is presented using artful and emotive language in order to appeal to both the reader's logic and emotions.*

This is introduction is not terribly long – only two sentences – but it accomplishes all of the goals of a good introduction:

- It provides context for the essay by introducing the passage in question

- It includes the name of the author and the article

- It summarizes the author's main claim and his purpose in writing, and it ends with the essay writer's thesis statement.

## HOMEWORK

**Directions:** In the last lesson, we looked at examples of language use drawn from a passage called "Why Mow? The Case Against Lawns." Today, we're going to use that passage to tie together some of the things we've learned about the SAT essay thus far. Read the passage as a whole. Use the lines provided to annotate the passage. You can look back at your assignment from lesson 5 when you evaluate the author's use of language, but you should also evaluate the author's use of evidence and logical reasoning. Finally, you will identify the persuasive techniques that you would include in an essay and write an introduction (including a strong thesis statement) for such an essay. *You don't need to write the whole essay.*

As you read the passage below, consider how Michael Pollan uses

- evidence, such as facts or examples, to support claims.
- reasoning to develop ideas and to connect claims and evidence.
- stylistic or persuasive elements, such as word choice or appeals to emotion, to add power to the ideas expressed.

**Adapted from "Why Mow? The Case Against Lawns" by Michael Pollan, published in *The New York Times*, May 28, 1989**

Nowhere in the world are lawns as prized as in America. In little more than a century, we've rolled a green mantle of grass across the continent, with scarcely a thought to the local conditions or expense. America has more than 50,000 square miles of lawn under cultivation, on which we spend an estimated $30 billion a year, according to the Lawn Institute, a Pleasant Hill, Tennessee, outfit devoted to publicizing the benefits of turf to Americans. Unfortunately, this vast green expanse is creating a host of environmental and health problems that are, like the lawn itself, unique to America.

Like the interstate highway system, like fast-food chains, like television, the lawn has served to unify the American landscape; it is what makes the suburbs of Cleveland and Tucson look more alike than not. France has its formal, geometric gardens, England its picturesque parks, and America this unbounded democratic river of manicured lawn along which we array our houses. Americans did not invent the lawn; lawns had been popular in England since Tudor times. But in England, lawns were usually found only on estates; the Americans democratized them, cutting the vast manorial greenswards into quarter-acre slices everyone could afford. The American lawn is an egalitarian conceit, implying that there is no reason to hide behind fence or hedge since we all occupy the same middle class.

However democratic a lawn may be with respect to one's neighbors, with respect to nature it is authoritarian. Under the mower's brutal indiscriminate rotor, the landscape is subdued, homogenized, dominated utterly. We superimpose our lawns on the land. And since the geography and climate of much of this country is poorly suited to turfgrasses (none of which are native), this can't be accomplished without the tools of 20th-century industrial civilization, with its chemical fertilizers, pesticides, herbicides, and machinery.

Need I point out that such an approach to "nature" is not likely to be environmentally sound? Lately we have begun to recognize that we are poisoning ourselves with our lawns, which receive, on average, more pesticide and herbicide per acre than any crop grown in this country. According to the EPA, 3 million tons of synthetic fertilizer and over 30,000 tons of pesticides are dumped on our lawns each year. Stories about the dangerous consequences of these lawn chemicals abound: Nearly 50 Ohio school children developed symptoms of poisoning after pesticides were sprayed at their school; seven dogs died after eating treated grass in an Oregon park; a Florida mother and her two children developed symptoms of acute poisoning immediately following lawn treatment.

Such stories are backed by clear evidence. A review of studies by the National Cancer Institute found a link between commonly used herbicides and cancers of the colon, lung, prostate, and ovary. The National Coalition for Pesticide Free Lawns reports that 19 of the 30 most commonly used lawn pesticides are known carcinogens. Companies that produce these chemicals are not required to list all ingredients on the labels, making it nearly impossible to identify the full dangers of these products.

Keeping off the lawn isn't a solution. Run-off from chemically treated lawns makes its way into the groundwater, ultimately winding up in rural wells and public water supplies. Researchers have found high concentrations of nitrates, which can cause several potentially fatal illnesses, in public water supplies throughout the country. This should hardly be surprising, given that half of America's bodies of water suffer from eutropication, or dead zones caused by oxygen-depletion brought on by excess algal growth due to high levels of nitrogen in the water.

If we are to maintain our democratic lawn, we must accept a degree of imperfection. The national obsession with the picture-perfect, weed- and pest-free carpet of lush, green grass has led to overuse of damaging chemicals, and weaning ourselves off of these chemicals will require that we live with a few weeds and bugs.

Should we prove unable to live with imperfect lawns, we may soon need to live without healthy lakes, rivers, and streams. We may need to live without venturing out of doors, since contact with chemical fertilizers and pesticides can be dangerous to our health. We may need to avoid using public water supplies. But at least we would have the comfort of knowing that our green space is immaculate, the envy of all the neighbors.

---

Write an essay in which you explain how Pollan builds an argument to persuade his audience that the prevalence of chemical lawn treatments creates environmental and health hazards. In your essay, analyze how Pollan uses one or more of the features listed above (or features of your own choice) to strengthen the logic and persuasiveness of his argument. Be sure that your analysis focuses on the most relevant features of the passage.

Your essay should not explain whether you agree with Pollan's claims, but rather explain how Pollan builds an argument to persuade his audience.

1.  Look at your passage annotation. Using your annotation, list the persuasive elements the author used in the passage:

    _____        _____

    _____        _____

    _____        _____

    _____        _____

2.  Let's build your thesis:

    a.  Introductory phrase: _____

    b.  Author's action: _____

    c.  Persuasive elements you'll discuss: _____

        _____

        _____

    d.  Effects of those persuasive elements: _____

        _____

        _____

    e.  Complete thesis statement: _____

        _____

        _____

        _____

3.  Now let's build your introduction:

    a.  Passage title and author's name: _____

        _____

    b.  Author's main claim and/or purpose: _____

        _____

        _____

    c.  Complete introduction (including thesis from #2): _____

        _____

        _____

        _____

        _____

        _____

        _____

        _____

## LESSON eB7 – PERSUASIVE ELEMENTS

**TOPIC OVERVIEW: PERSUASIVE ELEMENTS**

Regardless of the passage, all SAT essays will ask us to evaluate an author's arguments and the ways in which the author persuades his audience. To accomplish this task, a handy list of different means of persuasion would certainly be helpful.

Luckily, the Greek philosopher Aristotle came up with just such a list more than 2,000 years ago.

In 350 B.C., Aristotle wondered what could make a speech persuasive and memorable so that its ideas would pass from person to person. The answer, he argued, consisted of three principles: **ethos**, **pathos**, and **logos**. Content should have an ethical appeal, an emotional appeal, or a logical appeal. A speaker strong on all three was likely to leave behind a persuaded audience.

All these years later, writers and speakers still use these three persuasive elements to add power to their arguments. And because Aristotle's modes of persuasion are so widely used, it's likely that at least one – if not all three – of these persuasive elements will show up in nearly every passage on the essay section of the SAT.

**HOW DOES THIS HELP?**

If we already know that the passage will probably include at least one logical appeal, emotional appeal, or ethical appeal, we can look for these elements as we read the passage. Knowing how to spot examples of these persuasive elements will help us to quickly and easily identify parts of the passage that we can analyze in an essay.

> *Tip: Referencing Aristotle's elements of persuasion in your essay can also help you impress your reader by incorporating outside knowledge. For an example, check out Sample Essay D in Lesson 1.*

## ETHOS

*Ethos* refers to an ethical appeal – but probably not the type of ethical appeal that first comes to mind. Rather than appealing to the ethics of the *reader*, ethos is establishing the ethics of the *writer or speaker*. In essence, an argument rooted in ethos answers the question, "Is this person credible and trustworthy?"

Ethos is an effective persuasive strategy because when we believe that the speaker is credible and trustworthy, we are more willing to listen to what he has to say.

> *Consider this scenario:*
> Two doctors are debating the merits of a new drug called CureAll. Doctor A, who thinks that CureAll should undergo additional tests before being prescribed to patients, has spent his entire career working for a publicly funded research facility. Doctor B, who is in favor of immediately prescribing CureAll, once worked for the pharmaceutical company that developed the drug.

Which of these doctors is more credible and trustworthy (circle one)?

Doctor A                    Doctor B

Why did you choose this doctor?

_____

_____


When looking for elements related to ethos, look for words and phrases that suggest:

- trustworthiness
- credibility
- reliability
- expert testimony
- reliable sources
- fairness

Examples of ethos in a passage include:

- An author who shares his credentials in the field (such as a climate scientist writing about climate change)
- Use of expert testimony as evidence for a claim (such as quoting a climate scientist in a passage about climate change)
- Establishing reliable sources (such as citing a study from a university instead of citing a study from a for-profit or advocacy organization)
- Addressing counterarguments in order to demonstrate a fair assessment of all sides

## PATHOS

*Pathos* refers to emotional appeals. To remember this, think of *path*os and *path*etic, sym*path*etic, or em*path*etic.

When an author plays to a reader's emotions, the author is using pathos as a means of persuasion. For example, if an author is discussing the issue of homelessness, he might use a case study that follows the experience of a particular person. The case study itself might be used as evidence (which is an example of logos – more on that in a moment), but the way in which the author writes about the case study can also result in an argument rooted in pathos.

Consider these two excerpts:

*Excerpt A:*
Dasani, who lives with her family in the Auburn Family Residence, a city-run homeless shelter, is one of more than 22,000 homeless children in New York.

*Excerpt B:*
Dasani and her family live in the Auburn Family Residence, a decrepit city-run homeless shelter where mold creeps up the walls and roaches swarm. Beyond the shelter's walls, Dasani is part of a vast and invisible tribe of more than 22,000 homeless children in New York.

Both excerpts discuss the same homeless child, but they do so in very different ways. In excerpt A, the author sticks to the facts – where Dasani lives and how many homeless children are in New York. In excerpt B, the author adds descriptive words and phrases to tug at the reader's heartstrings. In the spaces below, list 3 words or phrases that make Excerpt B an argument rooted in pathos:

1. _____
2. _____
3. _____

What emotions does excerpt B create in the reader?

_____

_____

From a purely logical point of view, an argument rooted in pathos can be considered weak because it may not have actual evidence to support it. However, emotional appeals are often the most persuasive arguments. Many arguments are able to persuade people logically, but the audience may not follow through on taking action. Adding an emotional appeal compels people to listen and to act.

Arguments with elements of pathos often include:

- Descriptive words or phrases with emotional connotations (for example, "the child's **plight** was apparent in his **pinched, gaunt** face" versus "the child clearly suffered from malnutrition, as evidenced by his overly thin face")
- Personal stories that include emotional reactions
- Stories of individuals versus groups (for example, a case study of a single starving child has greater emotional impact than the results of a nationwide survey establishing the prevalence of childhood hunger)

## LOGOS

The Greek word *logos* is the basis for the English word logic, referring to a rational appeal that plays to the logical reasoning of the reader.

With the possible exception of very academic papers, most persuasive writing merges logos with some elements of pathos or ethos. This is because logic alone does not generally make for a very persuasive argument.

Consider these examples:

*Excerpt A:*
In 2005, the federal government spent $28.6 billion to fund the Supplemental Nutrition Assistance Program (SNAP), which provides food-purchasing assistance for low- and no-income individuals and families. By 2013, that number rose to $76.6 billion, which is in addition to the $10.1 billion spent on the National School Lunch Program, which feeds students whose families are at or below the poverty line. Despite increased spending on food assistance, childhood hunger is a growing problem: Today, 16.2 million children face food insecurity.

*Excerpt B:*
In 2013, the federal government spent more than $86 billion to provide food to low-income families. Although federal spending on nutrition assistance programs has more than tripled in the past decade, childhood hunger remains a growing problem. Today, nearly one in five children in America lives in a household that struggles to put food on the table.

Circle the excerpt that you believe rests solely on logos, without any elements of pathos or ethos.

Which excerpt do you find to be more persuasive? Why?

_____

_____

_____

Arguments rooted in logos often include:

- Facts
- Case studies (which often also include elements of pathos)
- Statistics
- Experiments or studies
- Logical reasoning (for example, "If we have already increased federal spending on food-purchasing assistance and the number of people without food has only continued to grow, then clearly additional federal spending isn't the solution.")
- Analogies
- Anecdotes (which often include elements of pathos)
- Authoritative sources (which often include elements of ethos)

## LOGOS, ETHOS, AND PATHOS IN PRESIDENT OBAMA'S ADDRESS TO THE NATION ON SYRIA

**Directions:** Persuasive speeches often utilize the same persuasive elements common to persuasive writing. Read the speech below, and then answer the questions to the right. Most of the questions deal specifically with logos, ethos, and pathos. Other questions provide additional examples of the types of language use and persuasive techniques that you might analyze in an SAT essay.

*On August 21, 2013, Syrian government forces under the leadership of President Bashar al-Assad used chemical weapons to massacre more than 1,400 men, women, and children in the suburbs of Damascus. People around the world witnessed these attacks via online videos and photos, leading to a global outcry and a call for international action. On September 10, 2013, U.S. President Barack Obama addressed the nation to outline his proposed response to the attacks in Syria. The following is an adaptation of his speech.*

My fellow Americans, tonight I want to talk to you about Syria, why it matters and where we go from here. Over the past two years, what began as a series of peaceful protests against the repressive regime of Bashar al-Assad has turned into a brutal civil war. America has worked with allies to provide humanitarian support, to help the moderate opposition, and to shape a political settlement.

But I have resisted calls for military action because we cannot resolve someone else's civil war through force, particularly after a decade of war in Iraq and Afghanistan.

1. Why do you think President Obama chose to open his speech with the phrase, "My fellow Americans"?

   _____

   _____

   _____

   _____

   _____

   _____

2. List two descriptive words or phrases that President Obama uses in the first paragraph to evoke an emotional response.

   _____

   _____

   _____

   _____

   _____

   _____

The situation profoundly changed, though, on August 21st, when Assad's government gassed to death over a thousand people, including hundreds of children. The images from this massacre are sickening: men, women, children lying in rows, killed by poison gas, others foaming at the mouth, gasping for breath, a father clutching his dead children, imploring them to get up and walk.

On that terrible night, the world saw in gruesome detail the terrible nature of chemical weapons and why the overwhelming majority of humanity has declared them off limits, a crime against humanity and a violation of the laws of war. Because these weapons kill on a mass scale, with no distinction between soldier and infant, the civilized world has spent a century working to ban them. And in 1997, the United States Senate overwhelmingly approved an international agreement prohibiting the use of such weapons, now joined by 189 governments that represent 98% of humanity.

On August 21st, these basic rules were violated, along with our sense of common humanity.

No one disputes that chemical weapons were used in Syria. The world witnessed their effects. And we know the Assad regime was responsible. We know Assad's troops were provided with gas masks before the attacks. We know senior figures in Assad's military machine reviewed the results of the attack.

When dictators commit atrocities, they depend upon the world to look the other way until those horrifying pictures fade from memory. But these things happened. The facts cannot be denied.

The question now is what the United States of America is prepared to do about it, because what happened to those people, to those children, is not only a violation of international law, it's also a danger to our security.

3. In the third paragraph, President Obama describes the chemical weapons attacks in Syria. How is his description an example of pathos?

_____

_____

_____

_____

_____

_____

4. Why do you think President Obama discussed the international efforts to ban chemical weapons? How does this information help make his argument stronger?

_____

_____

_____

_____

_____

_____

5. President Obama says that what happened "is not only a violation of international law, it's also a danger to our security." Why do you think he added the phrase about our security? Is this an example of logos, pathos, or ethos? Explain.

_____

_____

_____

_____

_____

_____

Let me explain why. If we fail to act, the Assad regime will see no reason to stop using chemical weapons. As the ban against these weapons erodes, other tyrants will have no reason to think twice about using poison gas. Over time our troops would again face the prospect of chemical warfare on the battlefield, and it could be easier for terrorist organizations to obtain these weapons to attack civilians.

This is not a world we should accept. This is what's at stake. And that is why, after careful deliberation, I determined that it is in the national security interests of the United States to respond to the Assad regime's use of chemical weapons through a targeted military strike. That's my judgment as commander in chief.

But I am also the president of the world's oldest constitutional democracy. So even though I possessed the authority to order military strikes, I believed it was right, in the absence of a direct or imminent threat to our security, to take this debate to Congress.

Now, I know that after the terrible toll of Iraq and Afghanistan, the idea of any military action, no matter how limited, is not going to be popular. It's no wonder, then, that you're asking hard questions. So let me answer some of the most important questions that I've heard from members of Congress and that I've read in letters you've sent me.

6. How is the paragraph that begins "Let me explain why" an example of logos? Would President Obama's argument be weaker if this paragraph were not part of the speech? Explain.

_____

_____

_____

_____

_____

_____

7. President Obama specifically refers to himself as "commander in chief" and "president of the world's oldest constitutional democracy." How are these references examples of ethos? How do they make President Obama's argument stronger?

_____

_____

_____

_____

_____

First, many have asked: Won't this put us on a slippery slope to another war?

My answer is simple. I will not put American boots on the ground in Syria. This would be a targeted strike to achieve a clear objective: deterring the use of chemical weapons and degrading Assad's capabilities.

Other questions involve the dangers of retaliation. We don't dismiss any threats, but the Assad regime does not have the ability to seriously threaten our military. Any other retaliation they might seek is in line with threats that we face every day.

Many have asked a broader question: Why should we get involved at all in a place that's so complicated and where those who come after Assad may also be enemies of human rights? It's true that some of Assad's opponents are extremists. But al-Qaida will only draw strength in a more chaotic Syria if people there see the world doing nothing to prevent innocent civilians from being gassed to death. The Syrian people and the Syrian opposition we work with just want to live in peace, with dignity and freedom. And the day after any military action, we would redouble our efforts to achieve a political solution that strengthens those who reject the forces of tyranny and extremism.

Finally, many of you have asked, why not leave this to other countries or seek solutions short of force?

I have a deeply held preference for peaceful solutions. Over the last two years, my administration has tried diplomacy and sanctions. But chemical weapons were still used by the Assad regime.

8.  President Obama addresses several counterarguments.

    True or False: In these paragraphs ("First, many have asked…still used by the Assad regime"), President Obama uses all three elements of persuasion.

    Circle one:

    TRUE            FALSE

    Explain your answer:

    _____
    _____
    _____
    _____
    _____
    _____
    _____
    _____
    _____
    _____
    _____
    _____
    _____
    _____
    _____
    _____

However, over the last few days, we've seen encouraging signs. The Russian government, an ally to Assad, has indicated a willingness to join the international community in pushing Assad to give up his chemical weapons. The Assad regime has now admitted that it has these weapons and even said they'd join the chemical weapons convention, which prohibits their use.

It's too early to tell whether this offer will succeed, but this initiative has the potential to remove the threat of chemical weapons without the use of force.

I have therefore asked the leaders of Congress to postpone a vote to authorize the use of force while we pursue this diplomatic path. We have been in discussions with Russian leaders, as well as the leaders of France and the United Kingdom. And we will work together in consultation with Russia and China to put forward a U.N. resolution requiring Assad to destroy his chemical weapons.

Meanwhile, I have ordered our military to maintain their current posture, to keep the pressure on Assad and to be in a position to respond if diplomacy fails.

9. These paragraphs contain the primary point of President Obama's speech. Summarize President Obama's primary argument using no more than two sentences.

_____

_____

_____

_____

_____

_____

My fellow Americans, for nearly seven decades the United States has been the anchor of global security. The burdens of leadership are often heavy, but the world's a better place because we have borne them.

And so I ask every member of Congress, and those of you watching at home tonight, the view those videos of the attack, and then ask: What kind of world will we live in if the United States of America sees a dictator brazenly violate international law with poison gas and we choose to look away?

Our ideas and principles, as well as our national security, are at stake in Syria, along with our leadership of a world where we seek to ensure that the worst weapons will never be used. When we can stop children from being gassed to death and thereby make our own children safer over the long run, I believe we should act. That's what makes America different. That's what makes us exceptional.

With humility, but with resolve, let us never lose sight of that essential truth.

Thank you. God bless you, and God bless the United States of America.

10. Towards the end of the speech, President Obama uses the phrase "my fellow Americans" for a second time. Why do you think he chose to repeat this phrase?

_____

_____

_____

_____

_____

11. In the final paragraphs of the speech, President Obama discusses the United States' role in the international community. How is this an example of pathos? How does this help to make President Obama's argument strong?

_____

_____

_____

_____

_____

12. Count the number of times that President Obama uses the words "children," "infants," or other similar terms. How is this repetition an example of pathos?

_____

_____

_____

_____

_____

## HOMEWORK

**Directions:** Read the essay prompt below. Use the space to the right of the passage to annotate the passage, and then answer the questions that follow. For extra practice, you may choose to write an essay using this prompt, but the essay is not required.

As you read the passage below, consider how Mac McClelland uses

- evidence, such as facts or examples, to support claims.
- reasoning to develop ideas and to connect claims and evidence.
- stylistic or persuasive elements, such as word choice or appeals to emotion, to add power to the ideas expressed.

**Adapted from "Schizophrenic. Killer. My Cousin." by Mac McClelland, published in *Mother Jones*, May, 2013**

On the other side of the visitors' glass, my cousin Houston looked surprisingly small and young for his 22 years. He possessed a remarkable vocabulary, vast, lovely, and lyrical. All things considered, he seemed altogether extremely unlike a person who had recently murdered someone.

Houston came home late one night in November 2011 and stabbed his father 60 times. In the preceding year, Houston displayed symptoms that have since been classified as "a classic onset of schizophrenia." When Houston began having violent outbursts, his psychiatrist told his parents, Mark and Marilyn, to call the police, the only option available given a lack of treatment facilities.

Eventually, Houston revealed his problems to our Aunt Annette. He suffered delusions that he was full of evil, that Mark was the source of the evil. But by then, it was too late.

Psychiatrist E. Fuller Torrey calls a crime like Houston's "a predictable tragedy." He applies the same term to the Gabrielle Giffords shooting, the Virginia Tech massacre, the Aurora movie theater shooting, and the Sandy Hook Elementary shooting. According to Torrey, such tragedies are entirely preventable, if only we provided adequate treatment for those who suffer from mental illnesses.

In 1773, the first North American facility for the mentally ill opened its doors. Over the next century, the rest of the country followed suit, taking "lunaticks" out of jail basements after Boston schoolteacher Dorothea Dix happened into one such dungeon and launched an activism rampage that led to the establishment of 110 public psych hospitals by 1880. By the 1950s, more than half a million people lived in US mental institutions.

Then, in 1961, a joint commission of the American Medical and American Psychiatric associations recommended integrating the mentally ill into society, replacing institutions with local facilities to provide outpatient care. Congress passed a law providing funding for such facilities, and states quickly dismantled their mental health hospitals. Between Vietnam

and an economic crisis, adequate funding for these facilities never materialized. In the 1980s, Reagan decreased federal mental-health spending by 30%, shifting the burden to the states. The result is a mental health system lacking both the large psych hospitals of the past and the community services that were supposed to replace them.

To many, this situation is a clear indication that deinstitutionalization was a mistake. Others worry that the return of institutionalization would result in the further victimization of the mentally ill. Cindy Gyori, executive director of Hyde Street Community Services, a San Francisco community mental-health center, says that whether they're in their "right mind" or not, mentally ill people should be able to do what they want until they're a danger – just like non-mentally-ill people. That violence has often already occurred by the time someone is forced to accept treatment is, Gyori says, a necessary "complication of our rights in America."

What of the studies that show that involuntary treatment laws reduce rates of violence, hospitalization, homelessness, and incarceration among severely mentally ill patients? Gyori calls such laws "stupid," adding that "it's the funding that matters." Funding for school screening programs that could catch early signs of mental illness, funding for early treatment to keep the moderately mentally ill from getting worse, and funding for intensive case management and subsidized housing for people who are functionally disabled. All things that combat the isolation, desperation, and hopelessness that can cause and exacerbate mental illness.

To those who claim that our age of austerity does not allow for such funding, Randall Hagar, director of government relations for the California Psychiatric Association, points out that the country will pay for it one way or another. "Taxpayers pay for nuisance issues related to the homeless," he says. "Two to three thousand dollars in treatment saves $50,000 in jail."

Indeed, by the time I visited Houston, he had been incarcerated for 430 days and had already cost the county $49,811 in jail expenditures alone. If there had been a facility – not a psych ward in a general hospital that is incapable of treating severe mental illness, but a clinic staffed with appropriate professionals and with an open bed and antipsychotics that have proven to be extremely effective if properly administered – if my Uncle Mark could have taken Houston to a place like that – maybe crimes like Houston's wouldn't happen so frequently.

"At least this story can go to a greater cause. I want people to know about this," Aunt Annette says, with a sharp, gasping cry. "If this story can serve a purpose, I feel like Mark will not have died in vain."

Write an essay in which you explain how McClelland builds an argument to persuade her audience of the necessity for changes in the ways in which we treat the mentally ill. In your essay, analyze how McClelland uses one or more of the features listed above (or features of your own choice) to strengthen the logic and persuasiveness of her argument. Be sure that your analysis focuses on the most relevant features of the passage.

Your essay should not explain whether you agree with McClelland's claims, but rather explain how McClelland builds an argument to persuade her audience.

1.  How is the author's story of her cousin an example of both ethos and pathos?

    _____

    _____

    _____

2.  How would the passage be less persuasive if the author had simply written about problems with mental healthcare without including the story of her cousin?

    _____

    _____

    _____

    _____

3.  How is the inclusion of a brief history of mental healthcare in America an example of logos?

    _____

    _____

    _____

4.  How does the inclusion of this history help to make the passage more persuasive?

    _____

    _____

    _____

    _____

5.  How is the author's use of expert testimony an example of both logos and ethos?

    _____

    _____

    _____

    _____

6.  How does quoting various experts help to make the author's arguments stronger?

    _____

    _____

    _____

    _____

7.  Why do you think the author chose to close the passage with a quote from her aunt?

    _____

    _____

    _____

    _____

8. List at least four words or phrases that demonstrate the use of pathos in the passage. For each word or phrase, briefly explain how that particular choice of words evokes emotion in the reader.

1) Word or phrase: _____

 Explanation: _____

 _____

2) Word or phrase: _____

 Explanation: _____

 _____

3) Word or phrase: _____

 Explanation: _____

 _____

4) Word or phrase: _____

 Explanation: _____

 _____

## LESSON eB8 – ORGANIZATION

**TOPIC OVERVIEW: ORGANIZATION**

In previous lessons, we've talked about how SAT essays are scored, how to evaluate the passages, and how to craft an introduction and a thesis. Now we're going to talk about how to put an essay together.

In the first lesson, we looked at the standards by which SAT essays will be graded. Those standards include:

- One clearly stated central claim that is maintained throughout the essay.
- A clear and effective introduction and conclusion.
- A logical progression of ideas.
- Consistent use of a variety of transitional strategies.

These are the things that we'll focus on today because these are the elements of a well-organized essay.

## CENTRAL CLAIM

The central claim of the essay will be the thesis statement. Remember that a good thesis statement should be specific, cover only what will be discussed in the essay, and appear in the first paragraph (the introduction) of the essay.

> *Tip: Review the Thesis Statement Recipe from Lesson 6 to remind yourself of the strategies for crafting a strong thesis statement.*

Although we've already learned how to write a good thesis statement, it's equally important that the ideas stated in the thesis statement *be maintained throughout the essay*. This is where organization comes in – by clearly organizing the essay, we can ensure that every paragraph of the essay relates back to the original claim.

## INTRODUCTIONS AND CONCLUSIONS

In Lesson 6, we discussed how to create good introductions. Remember that an introduction should include:

- The author's name and the name of the article
- The author's main claim and/or purpose
- Your thesis statement

Although the reader will already know the purpose and topic of the essay, a good writer always provides a solid introduction to provides context for everything that follows.

Because the SAT provides strict time limits, the introduction doesn't need to be incredibly fancy. As we discussed in Lesson 6, the introduction could be as little as two sentences long.

The same applies to the conclusion. A good writer never leaves the reader hanging. Even if there is only time to provide a one- or two-sentence-long conclusion, it is still important to provide closure to the essay.

An effective conclusion only needs to accomplish two tasks: 1) Summarize the main claim (using different wording than that of the thesis), and 2) tie the body paragraphs to that claim. A good example of this can be found in Sample Essay D from Lesson 1 of this book:

> **Thesis:** Using the concepts of ethos, pathos, and logos, Gioia constructs three interrelated arguments to conclude that the declining importance of literature in American society may well undermine the very fabric of our country.

> **Conclusion:** By utilizing all three forms of persuasive reasoning and relying on a wide variety of data-driven evidence, Gioia creates a strong argument in favor of acting to halt and reverse the decline of reading in the U.S.

Note that the thesis and the one-sentence conclusion are incredibly similar, yet they do not share the same wording. Note also that both sentences are linked to the body paragraphs, each of which discusses one or more of the three forms of persuasive reasoning.

## LOGICAL PROGRESSION OF IDEAS

How can we ensure that an essay written under strict time conditions will flow logically from one thought to the next?

The ideal way to achieve a logical progression of ideas is through properly planning the structure of an essay before writing. Many students are tempted to simply begin composition because they know they don't have much time to craft a compelling essay. This is a big mistake! The little time it takes to plan the essay is more than worth it because just a few moments of planning will result in a much more cohesive and logical essay.

> *Tip: Don't let the clock scare you – take the time to plan before you write!*

There is a trick to making planning fast and easy: Have a couple of potential essay structures in mind before test day. Although the passages provided will differ from test to test, the basic assignment will always be the same. We can use this to our advantage!

To plan an essay quickly, begin by reading and annotating the passage. This helps to identify all of the most important aspects of the author's arguments, which makes it easier to quickly decide on an essay structure.

We have three potential basic essay structures that will work for just about any SAT essay. Let's look at them.

*STRUCTURE ONE: EVALUATING ARGUMENTS AND LANGUAGE*

In Lesson 2, we talked about how to evaluate arguments, focusing strongly on use of evidence and logical reasoning. In Lesson 5, we talked about evaluating an author's use of language. By combining these lessons, we can develop a basic essay structure that looks like this:

      <u>Paragraph One</u>: Introduction with thesis statement.
      <u>Paragraph Two</u>: Evaluate a piece of evidence and its connection to an argument.
      <u>Paragraph Three</u>: Evaluate a second piece of evidence and its connection to an argument.
      <u>Paragraph Four</u>: Evaluate the author's use of language overall, citing specific examples in the paragraph.
      <u>Paragraph Five</u>: Conclusion.

*STRUCTURE TWO: ARISTOTLE'S MODES OF PERSUASION*

In Lesson 7, we learned about Aristotle's Modes of Persuasion – logos, ethos, and pathos. As we mentioned in that lesson, these three persuasive elements will appear in some combination in just about every essay passage. We can use the modes of persuasion as a possible essay structure by following this outline:

      <u>Paragraph One</u>: Introduction with thesis.
      <u>Paragraph Two</u>: Evaluation of use of logos, citing specific examples from the passage.
      <u>Paragraph Three</u>: Evaluation of use of pathos, citing specific examples from the passage.
      <u>Paragraph Four</u>: Evaluation of use of ethos, citing specific examples from the passage.
      <u>Paragraph Five</u>: Conclusion.

*STRUCTURE THREE: LINE BY LINE*

This particular structure has some definite pros and cons. On the one hand, it's by far the fastest of the three structures in terms of planning. On the other hand, this structure makes it more difficult to focus the essay on just a few of the key elements of the passage, which can be a big disadvantage on a timed essay. To use this structure effectively, it is important to first eliminate those elements that have little bearing on the main claim.

Note that this basic outline might be longer or shorter depending on how many arguments the author included in the passage:

> Paragraph One: Introduction with thesis.
> Paragraph Two: Evaluation of the author's first argument.
> Paragraph Three: Evaluation of the author's second argument.
> Paragraph Four: Evaluation of the author's third argument.
> Paragraph Five: Conclusion.

*USING THE STRUCTURES TO PLAN*

Any one of these three structures can be used to craft a cohesive essay, so choosing a structure is largely a matter of personal preference.

Keep in mind, however, that some passages may lend themselves more readily to one structure over another. For example, some passages may focus very heavily on evidence, in which case the first structure may be the easiest to work with. Other passages may contain very clear and obvious examples of logos, pathos, and ethos, which could make that particular essay structure both easier and more effective. And still others may not have an easily discernable pattern of persuasion, in which case the third structure might be the best option.

> *Tip: Familiarize yourself with all three basic essay structures, but try to find the one that you're most comfortable with when you write practice essays.*

After reading and annotating the passage, determine which of the three structures best suits the essay. Since the structure will determine the ideas presented in the body paragraphs, the structure will inform the thesis statement.

For example, if we know we're going to use the evidence/language approach, the thesis statement will need to specify that the essay will evaluate the author's use of evidence and language. If, on the other hand, we plan to use the logos/ethos/pathos approach, the thesis statement will need to specify that the essay will evaluate the author's use of these three modes of persuasion.

After deciding on the structure, use the Thesis Statement Recipe from Lesson 6 to craft a thesis statement. It's important to create your thesis statement before planning the rest of the essay because the rest of the essay has to relate back to the thesis statement.

Next, take just one minute to jot down the main idea of each body paragraph. Make sure the main ideas of the body paragraphs relate to the thesis. Using the chosen structure, create a simple list:

1. Thesis statement/Introduction
2. Main idea of body paragraph one
3. Main idea of body paragraph two
4. Main idea of body paragraph three
5. Conclusion

Given the time constraints, there's no point spending valuable minutes creating a detailed outline of the essay. It takes just a few seconds to create a sketchy list of main ideas, and those few seconds will pay off by saving time while writing and by helping to ensure that the essay is cohesive and well-organized.

*To Recap:*

1. Read and annotate the passage.
2. Pick an essay structure to use.
3. Write your thesis statement.
4. List the main ideas of each body paragraph.

## PULLING IT ALL TOGETHER

**Directions:** It's time to put this strategy to use. Using the passage below, follow the four planning steps we just reviewed: 1) Read and annotate the passage; 2) Decide on a structure; 3) Write your thesis; 4) List the main ideas of each body paragraph. Use the lines provided to the right of the passage to annotate the passage. Then complete the exercises that follow.

As you read the passage below, consider how James Hamblin uses

- evidence, such as facts or examples, to support claims.
- reasoning to develop ideas and to connect claims and evidence.
- stylistic or persuasive elements, such as word choice or appeals to emotion, to add power to the ideas expressed.

**Adapted from "Art Is Vital," by James Hamblin, published June 28, 2014 in *The Atlantic.***

In 2011, a spectacular video of Lil Buck dancing to Yo-Yo Ma brought jookin – a form of street dance that draws from hip-hop, ballet, jazz, and modern dance – into the mainstream. Ma would later call Buck a genius – and he is. According to the theory of multiple intelligences, Buck is off the charts in intelligences like spatial, musical/rhythmic, and bodily/kinesthetic.

The theory of multiple intelligences was developed in 1983 by Howard Gardner, who is now the Hobbs Professor of Cognition and Education at Harvard. It defines intelligence as a set of skills that make it possible for a person to solve problems in life. It's a far more expansive definition than many curricula address, and some of the multiple intelligences are routinely ignored in traditional schools.

Buck, whose given name is Charles Riley, was born in Chicago but grew up in Memphis. He recalls his education without nostalgia. "It wasn't all that good for me. I got made fun of a lot because I have big ears. Everybody called me Dumbo. This was before I was dancing. I'd be so focused on trying to handle that situation, I didn't really listen to the teachers."

Like Buck, jookin is a product of Memphis. Buck picked up the unique dancing style on the playground, before he transferred to a fine arts high school to study hip-hop and ballet, and dancing became his life. Now 26, he performs at benefits and works with children to advocate the arts in education.

Throughout the nineteenth century, Gardner notes, arts education – drawing, music, literature, drama, dance – were seen as instrumental to a student's overall development. But today, "there's a heightened pressure for proof that it's worth having something in the curriculum. With so many disciplines struggling for space, the arts can be an endangered species."

In surveys, Americans generally say they support liberal arts in education. But in terms of budgets, it is not math and science departments – or even

athletics departments – that get cut first. It's the arts. According to a review by Grantmakers in the Arts, when adjusted for inflation, total government funding for art education has declined by 31% in the past two decades.

Minimizing the arts' role in education, explains Damian Woetzel, director of the Aspen Institute Arts Program, "came about in a frame of increased emphasis on test scores and utility – the market economy becoming a marketing society. Everything is about what you're going to get," in readily quantifiable terms.

Studying visual art, dance, theater, and other forms of art doesn't typically result in a higher SAT score or a lucrative career, so by today's standards of worth, such subjects are seen as surplus. When the value of a field is defined by such narrow, concrete terms, it becomes far easier to cut these supposedly worthless school programs. But Woetzel argues that art education can "give kids the tools to become adults who are creative, adaptable, and collaborative, expressive – capable of having their eyes and ears and senses alive."

It was Woetzel who programmed Lil Buck's now infamous performance of "The Swan" with Ma in 2011. Today, the two collaborate in bringing arts into schools, working directly with students.

"We're not talking about making sure that everybody has private music lessons," Woetzel says. "We're talking about a way of educating that involves artistic habits of mind. The ability to re-assess and to imagine. To be in a science class and not think it's about memorization entirely," but to imagine its applications.

Indeed, several studies support the idea that arts education improves cognition, resulting in better and more efficient learning in other subject areas. A series of studies conducted by the Dana Foundation in 2004 found, among other things, that musical training improves the brain's ability to manipulate information, practicing performance art improves memory, and studying dance improves observational learning. To ignore the valuable impact that art can have on neurological development is to unforgivably limit students' potential.

While it's true that learning to paint, sculpt, dance, act, or play an instrument may not tangibly help a student to become an engineer or a doctor, studying art facilitates the learning of everything else. Art truly does make students smarter – just as it makes them more creative, innovative, and able to collaborate. And in an age in which those very traits are in great demand, can we truly afford to ignore the arts in our schools?

Write an essay in which you explain how Hamblin builds an argument to persuade his audience of the importance of art education. In your essay, analyze how Hamblin uses one or more of the features listed above (or features of your own choice) to strengthen the logic and persuasiveness of his argument. Be sure that your analysis focuses on the most relevant features of the passage.

Your essay should not explain whether you agree with Hamblin's claims, but rather explain how Hamblin builds an argument to persuade his audience.

**Step Two: Decide on a Structure**

Look over the notes you made while you annotated. Does the passage lend itself to a particular essay structure? If not, simply choose the essay structure you feel most comfortable using.

Which essay structure will you use (circle one):

- A. Evaluating Arguments and Language
- B. Logos, Pathos, and Ethos
- C. Line by Line

Write one to two sentences explaining why you chose this structure. Why do you think the passage lends itself to this particular structure, or why do you feel most comfortable using this structure?

_____

_____

_____

**Step Three: Write Your Thesis Statement**

Now we're going to use the Thesis Statement Recipe to craft your thesis. If you don't remember how to use the Thesis Statement Recipe, look back at Lesson 6 in this book.

1. Introductory phrase: _____

2. Author's action: _____

3. Persuasive elements you'll discuss: _____

   _____

   _____

4. Effects of those persuasive elements: _____

   _____

   _____

5. Complete thesis statement: _____

   _____

   _____

   _____

**Step Four: List the Main Ideas of Your Body Paragraphs**

You've got a structure and a thesis. Now list the main ideas of each body paragraph. Remember that the main idea of each body paragraph needs to relate back to your thesis!

1.  Paragraph One: Introduction with thesis.

2.  Paragraph Two: _____
    _____
    _____

3.  Paragraph Three: _____
    _____
    _____

4.  Paragraph Four: _____
    _____
    _____

5.  Paragraph Five (optional): _____
    _____
    _____

6.  Paragraph Six: Conclusion

## TRANSITIONAL STRATEGIES

The final grading standard for organization is "Consistently uses a variety of transitional strategies." Most writers understand basic transitions – first, second, next, finally, and so on – but transitional strategies go far beyond the mere memorization and use of a list of transitions and transitional phrases to include multiple writing practices that help the reader follow the logic of a writer's ideas. Let's review some of these strategies.

*TRANSITIONS WITHIN PARAGRAPHS*

Most essay writers attempt to include transitions in between paragraphs, but too often, they ignore transitions within paragraphs. This is a big mistake!

An effective paragraph must have both **unity** and **cohesion**. A unified paragraph sticks to one topic from start to finish, with every sentence contributing to the central purpose and main idea of that paragraph. But a string of sentences on the same topic doesn't really result in a good paragraph. Those sentences need to be clearly connected in order to tell readers how one detail or thought leads to the next. A paragraph with clearly connected sentences is said to be cohesive. Strong paragraphs are both unified and cohesive.

Let's look at an example. Both of the following paragraphs are unified – they both argue the benefits of a messy room. But the first paragraph lacks cohesion. <u>As you read the second paragraph, circle or underline the transitional words and phrases that help the paragraph flow</u>.

*Paragraph A*

I have a messy bedroom, and I'm not ashamed to admit it. I find it important to note the important distinction between "messy" and "dirty." A dirty bedroom features unpleasant smells, food that has turned into science experiments, and possibly (probably) critters. A messy bedroom is sanitary but seemingly disorganized. This last phrase – "seemingly disorganized" – is a bone of contention between my mother and I. My mother believes that it is impossible to find anything in my messy bedroom. I have far greater difficulty finding things when my room has been recently cleaned. I am so habituated to the practice of simply remembering where and when I last saw a given item that I find it much easier to locate things in a room that hasn't been reorganized and rearranged. I have an excellent memory, which will certainly help boost my SAT score. My mother should be glad of my messy room and its memory enhancing powers.

*Paragraph B*

I have a messy bedroom, and I'm not ashamed to admit it. To begin with, I find it important to note the important distinction between "messy" and "dirty." A dirty bedroom features unpleasant smells, food that has turned into science experiments, and possibly (probably) critters. A messy bedroom, on the other hand, is sanitary but seemingly disorganized. This last phrase – "seemingly disorganized" – is a bone of contention between my mother and I. My mother believes that it is impossible to find anything in my messy bedroom. On the contrary, I have far greater difficulty finding things when my room has been recently cleaned. In fact, I am so habituated to the practice of simply remembering where and when I last saw a given item that I find it much easier to locate things in a room that hasn't been reorganized and rearranged. As a result, I have an excellent memory, which will certainly help boost my SAT score. Thus, my mother should be glad of my messy room and its memory enhancing powers.

*TRANSITIONS BETWEEN PARAGRAPHS*

Transitions between paragraphs are just as important as transitions within paragraphs, and most students already know this. That said, the transitions between paragraphs need to be much more subtle and better integrated than the standard "first, second, third, in conclusion" that we often see in essays.

> *Tip: Avoid relying on transitional words or phrases when transitioning between paragraphs – link the ideas of the paragraphs instead.*

Instead of treating paragraphs as separate ideas, transitions between paragraphs can help readers understand how paragraphs work together, reference one another, and build to a larger point. The key is to highlight the connections between paragraphs by continuing one paragraph where another leaves off. Get away from the standard, clunky transitions you've memorized and start using *ideas* to link your paragraphs. Using key phrases or ideas from the previous paragraph helps to create a smooth and logical progression for a reader.

*Example of Clunky Transitions:*

Throughout the first half of the nineteenth century, Northern and Southern states followed vastly different patterns of economic development. The North, which had a shorter growing season and less fertile soil than the South, was ill-suited to agriculture and instead developed a thriving manufacturing sector. The South, on the other hand, had enjoyed a successful agrarian economic model for so long that Southerners found manufacturing to be largely unnecessary.

**Secondly, each region relied on a different type of labor**. The Southern plantations that largely fueled the region's economy were made possible only by the use of slave labor, an abhorrent practice that has long been condemned in the history books.. Northern manufacturers relied on immigrant labor, which was disconcertingly similar in that workers operated under terrible conditions and for very little recompense.

*Example of Smooth Transitions:*

Throughout the first half of the nineteenth century, Northern and Southern states followed vastly different patterns of economic development. The North, which had a shorter growing season and less fertile soil than the South, was ill-suited to agriculture and instead developed a thriving manufacturing sector. The South, on the other hand, had enjoyed a successful agrarian economic model for so long that Southerners found manufacturing to be largely unnecessary.

**These contrasting economic models resulted in reliance on different types of labor**. The Southern plantations that largely fueled the region's economy were made possible only by the use of slave labor, an abhorrent practice that has long been condemned in the history books.. Northern manufacturers relied on immigrant labor, which was successful largely because workers operated under terrible conditions and for very little recompense.

> *Tip: Instead of writing transitions that could connect any old paragraph to any other paragraph, create transitions that can ONLY connect these specific paragraphs.*

*TRANSITIONAL SENTENCES OR PARAGRAPHS*

If we're no longer relying solely on transitional words and phrases, we need something to replace them with. That's where transitional sentences and paragraphs come in. In fact, the example of smooth transitions that we just looked at is an example of a transitional sentence.

A transitional sentence can appear at the beginning or end of a paragraph. If it appears at the beginning of the paragraph, it should be linking the ideas in that paragraph with the ideas in the previous paragraph (like in the example of smooth transitions). If it is at the end of the paragraph, the transitional sentence should be linking the ideas in that paragraph with the ideas in the next paragraph.

But we can go even bigger than a transitional sentence. We can even use transitional paragraphs.

A transitional paragraph can be just a single sentence that stands on its own, or a multi-sentence paragraph that illustrates the complex connection between two other paragraphs. Single-sentence transitional paragraphs are often used for emphasis or to explain the connection between two paragraphs when simpler techniques just won't work. Multi-sentence transitional paragraphs are usually reserved for instances in which the connection between two paragraphs is just too complex to clearly explain in just one sentence.

> *Tip: In your SAT essays, you should mostly rely on transitional sentences to link paragraphs. This provides a smooth and logical flow of ideas while avoiding the gracelessness of common transitional words and phrases. Reserve transitional paragraphs for truly complex connections.*

Let's use the same paragraphs we just looked at to see an example of this:

> Throughout the first half of the nineteenth century, Northern and Southern states followed vastly different patterns of economic development. The North, which had a shorter growing season and less fertile soil than the South, was ill-suited to agriculture and instead developed a thriving manufacturing sector. The South, on the other hand, had enjoyed a successful agrarian economic model for so long that Southerners found manufacturing to be largely unnecessary.
>
> **Both the Southern agrarian economy and the Northern manufacturing economy required a ready supply of cheap labor, and although the cultural heritages of each region resulted in different solutions to this issue, both regions committed atrocities in the name of economic success.**
>
> The Southern plantations that largely fueled the region's economy were made possible only by the use of slave labor, an abhorrent practice that has long been condemned in the history books. Northern manufacturers relied on immigrant labor, which was disconcertingly similar in that workers operated under terrible conditions and for very little recompense.

## HOMEWORK

**Directions:** Use the lines provided to write an essay in response to the prompt that you annotated during class. You have already read and annotated the prompt, decided on an essay structure, written a thesis statement, and planned your body paragraphs. Use what you've learned about transitions to focus on the smooth logical flow of your essay. Although you won't be timed, you should limit yourself to no more than 25 minutes in writing this essay.

## LESSON eB9 – STYLE AND TONE

### TOPIC OVERVIEW: STYLE AND TONE

In all of the previous lessons, we've established the bones of an essay – the content and how to organize it – but we haven't really touched on the details of the essay.

The SAT essay section is designed to evaluate several fundamental skills sets: reading comprehension, analysis, and writing. To demonstrate strong writing skills, it is important to focus not only on *what* is written, but also on *how* it is written.

That's where style and tone come in.

In the first lesson, we looked at the standards by which the essays will be graded. Those standards include:

- Establishes and maintains formal and informative style
- Uses precise language consistently, including descriptive words and phrases, linking and transitional words, and words to indicate tone.

These are the things that we'll focus on today because these are some of the elements of a well-written essay.

### STYLE AND TONE: WHAT'S THE DIFFERENCE?

When discussing writing, style and tone are often used interchangeably, so it might seem as if they're the same thing.

They aren't!

**Style** is the way in which something is written. When it comes to nonfiction writing – like your SAT essays – writers are generally limited to just two options: formal and informal. (Nonfiction academic writing is not, after all, known for its humor or creativity.) Since the grading standards for the essay specifically say "formal and informative style," we already know what we should be shooting for.

**Tone** describes the author's attitude toward the subject and audience. In the case of an SAT essay, it is important that the tone of the essay demonstrates that the writer takes the assignment seriously, has respect for the audience, and is confident while writing.

For the purposes of the essay, we don't really need to know the difference between the two – we just need to know what the goals are. (Unless, of course, the passage for the SAT essay discusses style and tone…)

> *Tip: Don't worry about parsing the definitions of style and tone. Just remember: Your essay should show that you take the assignment seriously, that you have respect for your audience, that you're confident while writing, and that you can properly use a formal and informative writing style.*

## WHAT ABOUT DICTION?

Diction is part of this whole style/tone thing because word choices will establish the style and tone. Let's look at some examples:

| | |
|---|---|
| **Formal** | Are not angry |
| **Informal** | Aren't mad |
| **Positive** | The politician's stance |
| **Negative** | The politician's spin |
| **Taking the assignment seriously** | The author's arguments could be stronger. |
| **NOT taking the assignment seriously** | The author's arguments are stupid. |

These examples demonstrate how the choice of words can create a specific style or tone. Remember that it is important to "use precise language" in order to create the appropriate style and tone in the essay.

## FORMAL VS. INFORMAL

To use formal style in essay writing, a good writer needs to be able to tell the difference between formal and informal writing. Here are some quick rules to help define each writing style:

| | Informal | Formal |
|---|---|---|
| **Contractions** | Acceptable<br><br>*Example: The author doesn't just rely on evidence.* | NOT acceptable<br><br>*Example: The author does not rely solely on evidence.* |
| **Slang/Colloquial** | Acceptable<br><br>*Example: The author argues that kids should read more.* | NOT acceptable<br><br>*Example: The author argues that children should read more frequently.* |

| | | |
|---|---|---|
| **Person** | 1st and 2nd person acceptable<br><br>*Example: The author tries to convince you…*<br>*OR*<br>*I think the author's arguments are strong.* | ONLY use 3rd person<br><br>*Example: The author tries to convince his readers…*<br>*OR*<br>*The author's arguments are strong.* |
| **Sentence Structure** | Short, simple sentences acceptable<br><br>*Example: The author uses creative language. This language creates a humorous tone.* | Use varied sentence structures; emphasis on longer, more complex sentences<br><br>*Example: The author utilizes creative language to establish a humorous tone.* |
| **Diction** | Simplistic word choices acceptable<br><br>*Example: Although it sounds weird…*<br>*OR*<br>*The author hides the problems in his argument.* | Requires use of higher level vocabulary<br><br>*Example: Though it may seem strange…*<br>*OR*<br>*The author obscures the inconsistencies in his argument.* |

## PRACTICE WITH CONSISTENT STYLE

**Directions:** The following paragraph has several inconsistencies in its style. On the lines provided, rewrite the paragraph to create a consistent, formal style.

When writing a term paper, the one thing you've got to remember is to use authoritative sources. These are vital if the paper is to persuade the intended audience. Reliable sources can be found everywhere from the library down the street to the internet. Internet sources must be used cautiously, since some sites are just run by wackos; nonetheless, some sites do provide quality information. Once you have found your sources, the writer must remember to cite them properly in order to avoid plagiarism. Plagiarism is bad. Citation styles vary across the disciplines, but they can usually be figured out if you use a proper style manual.

## INFORMATIVE STYLE

The grading standards say to use a formal and **informative** style. So what's an informative style? These writing styles should seem familiar from prior English classes:

- Descriptive: Focuses on describing something in great detail; often rather poetic
- Persuasive: Attempts to persuade the reader to agree with the author's opinions or beliefs
- Narrative: Generally tells a story, usually from the author's point of view
- Expository/Informative: Explains a certain topic or subject to the reader without bias or personal opinions

Pay particular attention to that last type of writing because this is what is expected on the SAT essay.

Interestingly, the previous incarnation of the SAT essay was a persuasive writing assignment. The creators of the most recent version of the SAT kept a certain element of persuasive writing in the essay section by making the passages examples of persuasive writing, but instead of asking students to demonstrate persuasive writing skills, they are now asking students to demonstrate their *knowledge* of persuasive writing skills.

Since the SAT essay forms a bridge between persuasive and informative writing, it is essential to be familiar with both forms. Let's look at some of the elements of persuasive language that we introduced in Lesson 5 and compare them to the elements of informative language.

|  | **Persuasive** | **Informative** |
|---|---|---|
| **Formal/ Informal** | Can use whichever style is most likely to persuade a reader. | Should only use **formal** language, which establishes your authority on the subject matter. |
| **Inclusive/ Exclusive** | Often uses inclusive language to establish a connection with the reader. | Should only use third person, which is **exclusive**, in order to establish an impersonal and unbiased tone. |
| **Emotive Language** | Often uses emotive language to appeal to the reader's emotions. | Relies solely on impersonal, unemotional language in order to remain unbiased. |
| **Figurative Language** | Often uses figurative language (similes, metaphors, etc.) to emphasize or develop persuasive arguments. | Does not use figurative language in order to avoid any trace of bias or emotion. |
| **Humor** | May use humor to either persuade or connect with the reader. | Avoids humor in order to maintain an authoritative, serious tone. |

In looking at this chart, we can see a general pattern: Persuasive writing uses pretty much any means available to persuade and connect with the reader, while informative writing remains very impersonal and disconnected.

> *Tip: It's all about distance. In persuasive writing, you want to be close to your readers, sitting right next to them and sharing a joke. In informative writing, you want to maintain distance from your reader, like a professor lecturing to a big group of students. On the SAT essay, you're a professor in front of a lecture hall.*

## PRACTICE WITH PERSUASIVE AND INFORMATIVE LANGUAGE

**Directions:** Label each of the following as either PERSUASIVE or INFORMATIVE and explain your answer. If the sentence(s) is persuasive, use the lines provided to rewrite the sentence(s) using an informative style.

EXAMPLE:

A big reason America is falling behind other countries in science and math is that we have effectively written off a huge chunk of our population as incapable of succeeding in them.

This is _Persuasive_.  Why?

*Uses inclusive language ("we") and less formal language that creates an emotional response ("effectively written off").*

If persuasive, rewrite the sentence using informative style:

*One reason America trails other countries in science and math is that a large segment of the population is considered to be incapable of succeeding in these fields.*

1.  According to the Census Bureau, although women make up nearly half the work force, they hold just 26 percent of science, technology, engineering or math jobs.

    This is _____.
    Why?

    _____

    _____

    If persuasive, rewrite the sentence using informative style:

    _____

    _____

    _____

    _____

2.  One in five college students are required to enroll in remedial courses before being allowed to take credit-bearing college courses, creating a situation in which underprepared students must borrow huge sums of money to take courses that don't help them to earn a college degree, all because their high schools failed to teach them basic knowledge and skills.

    This is _____.
    Why?

    _____

    _____

If persuasive, rewrite the sentence using informative style:

_____

_____

_____

_____

3.  The collective evidence from a number of similar studies suggests that bilingual abilities improve the brain's executive function, the command system that controls the processes for planning, problem solving, and performing several other mentally demanding tasks.

    This is _____.
    Why?

    _____

    _____

    If persuasive, rewrite the sentence using informative style:

    _____

    _____

    _____

    _____

4.  Given that recent research has found that bilingualism improves cognitive function, we must endeavor to provide bilingual education to our students in order to continue to lead in an increasingly global economy.

    This is _____.
    Why?

    _____

    _____

    If persuasive, rewrite the sentence using informative style:

    _____

    _____

    _____

    _____

5. As America's kids continue to fall behind, it's time to start asking whether a school calendar built for the 19th century is going to cut it in the 21st. Summer vacation might be fun, but there's nothing fun about the national economic decline that will surely result if we don't get our kids back on track.

This is _____.

Why?

_____

_____

If persuasive, rewrite the sentence using informative style:

_____

_____

_____

_____

## PRACTICE WITH STYLE/TONE

**Directions:** Now you're going to do something that you'll never get to do on the SAT: Revise your essay. Choose one of the practice essays that you've written in this book. On the lines below, rewrite your essay to create a "final draft." As you revise your essay, pay particular attention to the organization strategies we reviewed in Lesson 7 and the style and tone information we reviewed today. *Don't worry about changing or fixing your analysis – keep the content of the essay the same – just worry about polishing the organization, style, and tone of the essay.*

## HOMEWORK

**Directions:** Use everything you've learned about SAT essay writing to plan and write an essay on the prompt below. Although you won't be timed, you should try to limit yourself to no more than 50 minutes to read and annotate the passage and plan and write the essay.

As you read the passage below, consider how Susan Dominus uses

- evidence, such as facts or examples, to support claims.
- reasoning to develop ideas and to connect claims and evidence.
- stylistic or persuasive elements, such as word choice or appeals to emotion, to add power to the ideas expressed.

**Adapted from "Is Giving the Secret to Getting Ahead?," by Susan Dominus, published March 27, 2013 in** *The New York Times Magazine.*

Adam Grant is the youngest-tenured and highest-rated professor at the Wharton School of the University of Pennsylvania. He is also one of the most prolific academics in his field, organizational psychology, the study of workplace dynamics. Given his myriad accomplishments, Grant would seem to be the most efficient and productive member of a field that is dedicated to the study of efficiency and productivity.

Witnessing firsthand the sheer volume of Grant's commitments, and how he follows through on all of them, is an education in itself. Helpfulness is Grant's credo. He is the colleague who is always nominating another for an award or taking the time to offer a thoughtful critique or writing a lengthy letter of recommendation for a student. Grant often returns home to 200 unread e-mails – and he answers them all.

How does he do it? By giving to get ahead.

Organizational psychology has long concerned itself with how to design work so that people will enjoy it and want to keep doing it. Conventional thinking holds that employers should appeal to workers' self-interest: financial incentives, interesting work, or the possibility for advancement. Grant's research starts with a premise that turns this theory on its head: The greatest motivation is a sense of service to others. Grant argues that focusing on the contribution of our work to other people's lives actually makes us more productive than focusing on helping ourselves.

Grant first realized that his ideas might yield quantifiable results when he was a 22-year-old graduate student. He proposed a study set in a university fund-raising call center. Call centers are notoriously unsatisfying places to work: repetitive, emotionally taxing, and

unfulfilling. The manager had already tried the usual incentives – competitions or prizes – and was unimpressed with the results.

Grant's idea was different. Given that one of the center's primary purposes was funding scholarships, Grant brought in a student who had benefited from that fund-raising. The callers listened as the young man told them how much the scholarship had changed his life. A month later, the workers were spending 142% more time on the phone and bringing in 171% more revenue, even though they were using the same script. In a subsequent study, revenues soared by more than 400%. Even simply showing the callers letters from scholarship recipients increased their fund-raising abilities.

To Grant, what was most surprising was the fact that the callers actively denied the possibility that meeting a scholarship recipient had helped. They insisted that their improvements were the result of luck or greater experience. Eventually, having replicated the test five times, Grant was confident that he had eliminated alternative explanations. It was as if the good feelings had created a subconscious source of motivation.

In a separate study, Grant wanted to make the case that this type of prosocial behavior is applicable in corporate America as well. He studied workers at Borders who contributed to an employee-beneficiary fund managed by the staff, with Borders matching donations. The money was set aside for employees in need. Interestingly, it was not the beneficiaries who showed the greatest increase in their commitment to Borders; it was the donors. Through interviews and questionnaires, Grant found that "as a result of gratitude to the company for the opportunity to affirm a valued aspect of their identities, they developed stronger affective commitment to the company."

Grant believes that part of the reason that giving contributes to success is that generosity requires willpower. He cites a study at Northwestern University that found that most people lose physical strength after enduring a test of will, like resisting cookies when hungry. Typically, the subjects could only squeeze a handgrip for 25 seconds after such an exercise. One group distinguished itself, squeezing the handgrip for 35 seconds. These were also people who Grant identified as "givers," those who habitually help others without expecting anything in return. "By consistently overriding their selfish impulses in order to help others, they had strengthened their psychological muscles, to the point where using willpower for painful tasks was no longer exhausting," writes Grant of the study.

For Grant, all of this is academic. He doesn't necessarily advocate implementation, but he finds the idea intriguing. Particularly in an age marked by unhappy workers – national surveys suggest that fewer than 19% of workers are satisfied with their jobs – the idea of encouraging productivity by encouraging generosity has merit. Yes, American workers have seen their wages stagnate, and that is a vital issue that must

Unauthorized copying or reuse of any part of this page is illegal.

be addressed. But money alone will not improve productivity or job satisfaction; perhaps giving to get ahead will.

---

Write an essay in which you explain how Dominus builds an argument to persuade her audience that generosity is a means to success and productivity. In your essay, analyze how Dominus uses one or more of the features listed above (or features of your own choice) to strengthen the logic and persuasiveness of her argument. Be sure that your analysis focuses on the most relevant features of the passage.

Your essay should not explain whether you agree with Dominus's claims, but rather explain how Dominus builds an argument to persuade her audience.

## LESSON eB10 – PUTTING IT TOGETHER

### TOPIC OVERVIEW: PUTTING IT TOGETHER

We've spent a lot of time talking about different parts of the essay – from reading and analyzing the passage to crafting a thesis and planning the essay. Today we'll put all of that knowledge together.

Before we begin, let's review the most important things to do to score well on the essay:

- Closely analyze the passage author's arguments
- Focus the essay on a single central claim
- Organize the essay so that it flows logically and smoothly
- Incorporate evidence from the passage in the essay
- Write in a formal, informative tone
- Avoid grammar, usage, and spelling errors

### LET'S REVIEW

**Directions:** The following questions review the concepts we covered in previous lessons. Answer each question without looking back in the book. If you get any questions wrong, go back and review the lesson that is associated with that question.

1. List two types of evidence that passage authors might use. (Lesson 2)

   _____

   _____

2. What should you do before you begin reading and annotating the passage? (Lessons 2 and 3)

   _____

   _____

3. How can repetition make an argument more persuasive? (Lessons 3 and 5)

   _____

   _____

4. In your own words, why is it important to annotate the passage? (Lesson 3)

   _____

   _____

5. When should you use quotations in your essay? (Lesson 4)

   _____

   _____

6. When should you paraphrase in your essay? (Lesson 4)

   _____

   _____

7. How does emotive language help to make an argument more effective? (Lessons 5 and 7)

   _____

   _____

8. What adjectives could describe a strong thesis statement? (Lesson 6)

   _____

   _____

9. In your own words, define ethos, pathos, and logos. (Lesson 7)

   _____

   _____

10. Which of the three essay organization structures do you feel most comfortable using and why? (Lesson 8)

    _____

    _____

11. Give an example of a sentence written in an informal style, and then rewrite that sentence in formal style. (Lesson 9)

    _____

    _____

## STEP-BY-STEP GUIDE TO TIMED SAT ESSAYS

Throughout the previous lessons, we've discussed various steps involved in crafting a strong SAT essay. We have already discussed most of these steps, but we haven't yet talked about how to time them. After all, there will only be 50 minutes to read and annotate the passage and plan and write the essay.

1. **Read the part of the prompt that follows the passage.** *< 1 minute*
   This part of the prompt will define the passage author's primary argument. Knowing the primary argument before reading the passage will help with identifying supporting arguments and evidence.
2. **Read and annotate the passage.** *15-20 minutes*
   - Underline the topic sentence or supporting argument in each body paragraph.
   - Circle or underline key words and phrases that might be incorporated into the essay.
   - Make notes in the margins to help keep track of evidence and persuasive elements.
3. **Choose an essay structure.** *< 1 minute*
   Decide which of the following essay structures will best suit the passage:
   - Arguments and language
   - Logos, pathos, ethos
   - Line by line
4. **Write the thesis and introduction.** *3 minutes*
   Use the Thesis Statement Recipe and the guidelines for creating an introduction, which can be found in Lesson 6 of this book.
5. **List the main ideas of each of the body paragraphs.** *3 minutes*
   Using the chosen essay structure to briefly identify the main idea of each body paragraph. Planning ahead will make writing go faster and ensure that the final essay is clear, cohesive, and logically organized.
6. **Write the essay!** *20-25 minutes*
7. **Take a moment to review and edit the essay.** *1-2 minutes*
   There won't be much time remaining, but it is important to *always* reserve one to two minutes to read through the essay to catch grammar, usage, and spelling errors.

## WRITING THE ESSAY

The steps above allow the writer to lay the groundwork for the essay. Although each of these steps will use valuable time, they will make writing the actual essay go much faster – so in the end, planning ahead saves time.

While writing the essay, keep the following tips in mind:

- Refer often to the annotations and list of body paragraph main ideas.
- Integrate evidence from the passage in the form of quotes or paraphrasing. Remember to only use quotes when there is a specific reason for quoting the passage – most of the evidence should be paraphrased.
- Utilize the transitional strategies that were discussed in Lesson 8. Don't rely on overly simplistic transitions like "first," "next," or "in addition."
- Pay close attention to the style and tone! The essay should be written in a formal and informative style, and the tone should demonstrate that the writer takes the assignment seriously and is a confident writer.
- Be careful to avoid grammar, usage, and spelling errors!
- Remember to include a brief conclusion – even a one-sentence conclusion is better than no conclusion at all.

## REVIEW YOUR ESSAY BEFORE TIME RUNS OUT

Yes, this is a timed writing assignment. Yes, it's more important to complete the essay than to complete the editing process.

But it's still worthwhile to leave just one or two minutes to review the essay.

Even if the writer is really, REALLY careful to avoid making errors in the essay, there will probably still be a few silly errors. It happens. The only way to make sure that those errors don't negatively impact the score is to read through the essay before the time runs out.

## LET'S PRACTICE

**Directions:** Use the steps to a strong essay to plan an essay on the following topic. We've provided some exercises to help guide your through several of the steps. During class, we're only going the plan the essay; you'll write the essay for homework. Don't forget the first step: Read the part of the prompt that follows the passage first!

As you read the passage below, consider how Maria Konnikova uses

- evidence, such as facts or examples, to support claims.
- reasoning to develop ideas and to connect claims and evidence.
- stylistic or persuasive elements, such as word choice or appeals to emotion, to add power to the ideas expressed.

**Adapted from "No Money, No Time," by Maria Konnikova, published June 13, 2014 in *The New York Times*.**

The absurdity of having had to ask for an extension to write this article isn't lost on me: It is, after all, a piece on time and poverty, about what happens when we find ourselves working against the clock. In the case of someone who isn't otherwise poor, poverty of time is just an inconvenience. For someone whose lack of time is just one many concerns, the effects compound quickly.

We make a mistake when we look at poverty as simply a question of financial constraint. When we think of poverty, we tend to think in monetary terms, but the financial part of the equation may not be the most important factor.

Take what happened with my request for an extension. It was granted, and the immediate time pressure was relieved. But now I'm struggling to dig myself out from the rest of the work that accumulated in the meantime. My experience is the equivalent of a high-interest loan, except instead of borrowing money, I borrowed time. This kind of borrowing comes with its own interest rate: By focusing on one immediate deadline, I neglect a whole host of other obligations. This is the same type of problem poor people encounter daily: The demands of the moment override the demands of the future, making that future harder to reach.

Sendhil Mullainathan, an economist at Harvard, says that "[t]here are three types of poverty. There's money poverty, there's time poverty, and there's bandwidth poverty." The first is the type we typically associate with the word. The second occurs when the time debt of the sort I incurred starts to pile up. And the third is the type of attention shortage that is fed by the other two: I make decisions that leave me worse off because I lack the resources to focus on anything other than what's staring me in the face at this exact moment.

When Edar Shafir, a psychologist at Princeton, first began studying poverty,

he assumed that the poor made the same mistakes in judgment as everyone else, except theirs ended up being more costly. He was wrong. "They were making mistakes that weren't the typical decision errors. They were worse," he recalls. "When you don't have enough, you focus on the little you have, and it leaves you with less attention."

In 2012, Mr. Shafir, Mr. Mullainathan, and Anuj Shah, a psychologist from the University of Chicago, tested how scarcity of the less-noticed kinds – time and bandwidth – affected decision-making ability and subsequent wealth. In the study, they randomly assigned participants either "poor" or "rich" conditions. The "poor" participants had less of a given resource – time, in some cases, or number of turns, in others. They then had everyone play several rounds of a game. Both the "rich" and "poor" players performed badly under certain circumstances, leading researchers to an interesting conclusion: Both scarcity and overabundance make us inefficient.

In three subsequent studies, Mr. Shafir and his colleagues made time their scarce resource. Players could use the time they were allocated, borrow with no interest, or borrow with twofold interest. When borrowing was an option, the "poor" borrowed more of their total budget than the "rich," regardless of interest rate. The more debt they acquired the more they borrowed. When researchers altered the variable to allow players to preview the next round's questions, the "rich" took advantage of the edge and strategized, while the "poor" acted as if they didn't see the previews at all. They were so focused on operating under scarcity that they couldn't strategize. "Scarcity, of any kind, will create a tendency to borrow," the researchers conclude.

The traditionally poor borrow money at high rates, but they must also borrow time. That's the invisible part of poverty that is missed: The poor are not just short on money; they spend their time worrying about all of their obligations and how they will meet them, leaving them without the mental bandwidth to make strategic long-term decisions.

If poverty is about time and mental bandwidth as well as money, how does this change our approach to the problem? It isn't enough to simply provide monetary resources to the poor. In order to break the cycle of poverty, we must also address a lack of time and mental bandwidth. By also finding ways to give the poor a metaphorical extension on their deadlines, we may just manage to give them enough breathing room to strategize and plan for the future, and that may make all the difference.

---

Write an essay in which you explain how Konnikova builds an argument to persuade her audience that policies that address poverty must go beyond providing monetary resources to the poor. In your essay, analyze how Konnikova uses one or more of the features listed above (or features of your own choice) to strengthen the logic and persuasiveness of her argument. Be sure that your analysis focuses on the most relevant features of the passage.

Your essay should not explain whether you agree with Konnikova's claims, but rather explain how Konnikova builds an argument to persuade her audience.

**Step One:** Read the part of the prompt that follows the passage to find out what the author's primary argument is.

**Step Two:** Read and annotate the passage. Consider which persuasive elements you want to use in your essay.

**Step Three:** Choose an essay structure based on the persuasive elements in the passage.

For this essay, I will use (circle one):

- Arguments and language
- Logos, pathos, ethos
- Line by line

**Step Four:** Build your introduction and thesis using the Thesis Statement Recipe.

*Thesis Statement Recipe:*

1. **Introductory phrase:** _____

2. **Author's action:** _____

3. **Persuasive elements you'll discuss:** _____

   _____

   _____

4. **Effects of those persuasive elements:** _____

   _____

   _____

5. **Complete thesis statement:** _____

   _____

   _____

   _____


*Build an Introduction:* Remember to include the passage title, author's name, and author's main claim.

_____

_____

_____

_____

_____

**Step Five:** List the main ideas of each of your body paragraphs.

1. Paragraph one: Introduction
2. Paragraph two: _____

   _____
3. Paragraph three: _____

   _____
4. Paragraph four: _____

   _____
5. Paragraph five (optional): _____

   _____
6. Paragraph six: Conclusion

## HOMEWORK

**Directions:** During class, you completed the planning stages for an essay – now it's time to actually write the essay. Since you're doing this at home, you don't be timed, but you should try to follow the timing guidelines that were explained in this lesson. Do your best to limit yourself to 20-25 minutes to write the essay and 1-2 minutes to review the essay for errors.

_____

_____

_____

_____

_____

_____

_____

_____

_____

_____

_____

_____

_____

_____

_____

_____

_____

_____

_____

_____

_____

_____

_____

_____

_____

_____

_____

_____

_____

_____

_____

_____

_____

_____